To Jock Blacklock and the late Mabel Blacklock, my amazing parents, with all my love. Two of your hallmark characteristics were responsibility and candor: you had wills and talked about them openly around the kitchen table as far back as I can remember. I thought about you both so much as I wrote this book.

JEAN

To my Dearest Aunt, Deirdre Romanes, who passed away during the writing of this book, with love. You will always be the bravest, strongest, most graceful and accomplished woman I have ever known.

SARAH

The 50 Biggest Estate Planning Mistakes . . . and How to Avoid Them

Jean Blacklock and Sarah Kruger

John Wiley & Sons Canada, Ltd.

Library and Archives Canada Cataloguing in Publication Data

Blacklock, Jean, 1961–

   The 50 biggest estate planning mistakes : and how to avoid them/Jean Blacklock and Sarah Kruger.

Includes index.
ISBN 978-0-470-68162-6

   1. Estate planning—Canada—Popular works.   I. Kruger, Sarah   II. Title.
III. Title: Fifty biggest estate planning mistakes.

KE5974.B52 2010   346.7105'2   C2010-903726-X
KF750.B52 2010

Production Credits
Cover design and interior text design: Natalia Burobina
Typesetter: Thomson Digital
Cover Image: George Diebold/Digital Vision/Getty Images
Printer: Friesens

John Wiley & Sons Canada, Ltd.
6045 Freemont Blvd.
Mississauga, Ontario
L5R 4J3

Printed in the United States of America

6 - 18

CONTENTS

PREFACE

THE IDEA FOR *The 50 Biggest Estate Planning Mistakes and How to Avoid Them* first occurred to Jean when she was practising estate law. It seemed to her then that the mistakes people make in estate planning are most often *not* because of some technical blooper or the oversight of an esoteric area of the law. Usually if people are doing complicated estate planning, they retain good professional help and all the provisions of the *Income Tax Act* are complied with, all the *t*'s crossed and the *i*'s dotted.

Instead, the mistakes that are made most often tend to be simple missteps or faulty assumptions, like thinking that the adult kids and spouses will magically get along after their parents' deaths, even though they don't really get along now, or being wilfully blind to the importance of specifying who will receive each piece of artwork. These types of common errors are not too glamorous, exciting or even necessarily of great monetary importance, but they can lead to months or even years of acrimony.

Jean's and Sarah's paths crossed during their time in financial services, at a point where Jean was responsible for wealth services and personal trusts at one of Canada's major banks and Sarah was working on a number of projects in the bank's wealth services area, requiring intensive interviews of Canadian and American families who were going through the succession-planning process. Jean's background and her interest in making complicated topics simple, and Sarah's ability to interview a wide range of subject matter experts, came together to enable them to write this book with the following objectives in mind: A book that would be fun and interesting to read, packed with useful tips and ideas from a swath of well-informed professionals whose work touches, one way or another, the professions of estate planning and estate administration.

The 50 Biggest Estate Planning Mistakes and How to Avoid Them falls into four sections. The first section contains the 7 Mistakes in planning for the possibility of mental incompetency; the second section discusses the 6 Mistakes that arise when no planning for death is done at all; the third section includes the 26 Mistakes that commonly happen when we do get around to our will planning; and the final section covers the 11 Mistakes that people make in the course of administering a deceased person's estate. A glossary at the back of the book defines terms that may be unfamiliar.

major themes

As we wrote the book, we were often asked by our family or friends, "*So*, what is the *biggest* mistake?" It is hard to even narrow it down to a Top 10 list, but we *can* say that most of the 50 Mistakes contain one of three themes:

1. procrastinating;

2. not taking the estate-planning process seriously enough; and

3. underestimating a possible problem and overestimating the people we love.

Procrastinating about estate planning is something a lot of people recognize in themselves, whether it's about preparing a first will or updating a later one. Planning for the possibility of our mental incompetency or the eventual certainty of our death is a tough and, at times, emotional process, which makes a trip to the dentist feel like a Caribbean vacation.

So, inevitably, some of the 50 Biggest Mistakes are about not getting important tasks done, not only the key documents such as powers of attorney for personal care (sometimes called personal or advance directives), powers of attorney for property, and wills, but also the organization of all our other papers in a manner that would be incredibly helpful to our executor when we die.

The second common thread throughout the mistakes is about *not taking estate planning seriously*. Mistake #14 is called "Is That Snoring We Hear?" and it discusses the phenomenon of people working on their estate planning mainly as a to-do item on the list, something to be stroked off the list like redoing the roof.

Although getting to the job can take some time (see above comments on procrastination!), once in the thick of it, people can err by pretending that this really won't be the "last" will. This attitude means that all those depressing questions about "who gets what when" are answered in a perfunctory way and it often results in mechanical reading and minimal comprehension of the draft documents prepared by the lawyer. *Why?* Because we delude ourselves into thinking that we will be doing another will in a few years and we promise ourselves to devote greater care and attention to it then. You can see where this attitude gets us: dying with a will that causes our loved ones to say, "*Really??* She really wanted *that*?"

Underestimating problems and overestimating the people we love is the third theme in the estate-related mistakes people make. People joke about mothers and fathers who can only see the good in their children and it is wonderful in life to have that unconditional and unfettered love that only parents give us. Having said that, when it comes to passing on the family cottage, leaving large sums of money with no strings attached, or putting our assets into joint names with only one of our children, mistakes happen, creating situations we never intended or imagined.

Mistake #31 is called "That's Not a Mosquito, That's Your Sister-in-Law," bringing to mind the exasperation we heard from many estate professionals as they reflected how there really are very few, if any, fail-proof ways to transfer the cottage from one generation to another. This difficulty is not about the legal or tax technicalities—those can be planned for—it is about the challenge of an expanding family over the years being able to work through individual foibles and interpersonal strife to achieve harmony in the usage of a single property, often laden with years of emotions.

Clearly, parents in doing their estate planning can underestimate the potential pitfalls throughout their overall estate plan, and at the same time overestimate the ability of the family "to work it out together" after Mom and Dad are gone.

a note about quebec

Although *The 50 Biggest Estate Planning Mistakes and How to Avoid Them* is not intended to be a technical book, it is based on Canadian law across the common law provinces and territories. In Quebec, the Quebec Civil Code provides much of the legal framework relating to estates, successions and trusts. While many of the general principles are the same as those in the common law provinces, the law in Quebec as it pertains to our topics of incompetency, wills, estates and trusts is different than in the rest of Canada and, for this reason, readers in Quebec will want to keep that cautionary note in mind.

Some topics covered in the book are relevant regardless of whether the common law or a civil code applies, coming from the anecdotes of trust and estate professionals in every province. These include keeping your estate planning current throughout the stages of your life, different ways to approach the treatment of personal effects, getting organized as an executor, and communicating effectively with the estate beneficiaries. Topics such as these will be relevant to readers anywhere in Canada, including Quebec. Just keep in mind that our references to provincial legislation do not include the legislation in Quebec, due to its significant differences.

ACKNOWLEDGEMENTS

WE WANTED THE BOOK TO reflect the experience of many estate and trust professionals across Canada, and we were fortunate to receive that assistance in a generous and unstinting way. We appreciated the immediate enthusiasm for our idea from family and friends, and from the professionals we spoke with, both those who were interviewed for the book and the many others whom we spoke with briefly about the manuscript. This support made the interviewing and writing of the book much more fun than we could have imagined at the outset of the project.

We are particularly grateful to the trust and estate professionals at BMO Trust Company, Royal Trust Corporation of Canada, The Bank of Nova Scotia Trust Company (ScotiaTrust) and The Canada Trust Company. We have listed the names of these professionals below. Representatives from these companies across the country shared their ideas with us by phone, and the Toronto-based professionals readily agreed to meet with us in person. Their insights enriched the entire book and particularly brought to life Section D of the book, which looks at the mistakes made in the course of estate administration.

We also are indebted to Nicole Woodward, a lawyer in Calgary, Alberta, who shares Jean's passion for estate law, both its technical details and its compelling human element. Nicole reviewed the entire manuscript, providing thoughtful and helpful suggestions on how to improve the book. Her time and attention to the manuscript no doubt enhanced the book considerably, but we hasten to add that any mistakes or oversights are entirely our own and we take full responsibility for them.

The following list includes the names of lawyers, mediators, chartered accountants, financial planners, physicians, social workers, nurses, trust officers, estate planners, executives and planned giving professionals in the charitable sector, and financial services executives who work in the areas of wealth services, insurance and philanthropy. Each of them gave generously of their time to speak with us and, in several cases, to read whole sections of the manuscript to provide us with their kind and helpful feedback on areas of their personal expertise.

In alphabetical order, the professionals who assisted us are:

Holly Allardyce, Joseph Bakish, Stephen Barrett, John Bathurst, Rahul K. Bhardwaj, Elaine Blades, Ann L. Brayley, Jeffrey Blucher, Lesley Cameron, Doug Clark, Daphne DeJong, Bernadette Dietrich, Vincent Daly, Patricia Daunais, Carol Edwards, Paul Fensom, Judy Fernandes, Angie Fong, Trevor Forrest, Ian Gergovich, Mary Goodfellow, Dr. Michael Gordon, Jerry Halma, Marni Hamilton, Elena Hoffstein, Jandy John, Leanne Kaufman, Barbara Kimmitt, Tony Lalonde, Richard Langford, Ross Lapointe, Dr. Margaret MacAdam, Peter McCarthy, Suzanne Michaud, Michael Murphy, Gillian Musk, Kirk O'Brien, Gerald Owen, Sharon Paterson, Gayle Pederson, Gaylanne Phelan, Sara Plant, Heidi Rankin, Philip Renaud, Anne Reynolds, Margaret E. Rintoul, Marvi Ricker, Rhonda Roberts, Keith Sjögren, Caroline Tapp McDougall, Kathy Tsenis, Janice Wells, Kimberly A. Whaley, Marni Whitaker, Michael Whitworth, and Sharon Wood.

In all cases where we have used an anecdote shared with us, we have taken care to change facts and details in order not to reveal the actual situation, so it is purely coincidental if the book contains names or descriptive facts that mirror or are similar to an actual situation or person, alive or dead. As well, although we credit our large number of supporters and participants with the book's practical flavour, we assume all responsibility for any error or omission.

personal thanks

Each of us is grateful for the encouragement we received in writing this book from our close friends and family. For Sarah's part, both her parents, Susan and Joseph, were a wonderful source for estate-related ideas, articles and encouragement; her dear friend, Hilary Drennan, proved once again that she can always be counted on for new perspectives on any issue; and Sarah's husband, Brian, never ceased to set aside what he was working on to lend an ear and offer suggestions.

Jean wishes to thank her terrific children—her sons, Tom Higa and Ted Higa, and her stepchildren, David Auerbach and Rebecca Auerbach—who are always interested in whatever she is working on; her long-time friend, Marilyn Paterson, who encouraged the writing of the book over many diner breakfasts; and her husband, Andrew, a big fan of the idea for "The 50 Biggest," who read every word and brought to the project his ability to make everything fun, even writing about wills and estates.

Last but certainly not least, we both wish to thank Karen Milner, the executive editor at John Wiley & Sons, Inc. (Canada), for her unreserved and enthusiastic encouragement from the very first mention of this book. We really appreciated Karen's strong support for our idea and her ongoing assistance with the writing and editing of *The 50 Biggest Estate Planning Mistakes and How to Avoid Them*. The entire team at John Wiley has been supportive, responsive, very interested in our project and always a pleasure to work with—thank you to all of you.

—*Jean Blacklock and Sarah Kruger*

PART 1

incompetency issues

WANTED: DEAD OR ALIVE!

MISTAKE #1

Failing to face the need to delegate your decision-making ability while you are still able to do so

AS WE RESEARCHED THE BOOK, this very first mistake of not planning for the possibility of mental incapacity was mentioned time and again in a heartfelt way. In speaking to us about being the delegated decision maker for his own mom, one seasoned trust professional said, "You know, I even had to decide if she should have a flu shot! Even though I have been in the trust and estate business for years, I had no idea what was really involved in the incompetency part of it. I wish Mom and I had talked about her views on the end of life before she became senile."

Making the mistake of not planning for incompetency is entirely normal in our society. We like to avoid thinking about being senile even more than we like to avoid thinking about our death. Flipping through a friend's photos of the River Ganges—where some of India's sick and elderly choose to die—makes us shudder and switch to talking about those Flames . . . or those Leafs . . . or how we got the bubble gum off the carpet!

In 2009, the Alzheimer Society of Canada released research noting that Alzheimer's disease and related dementias are *not* normal parts of aging and yet even so, in 2009, 1 in 11 Canadians over the age of 65 had Alzheimer's disease or some form of mental disorder. As the baby boomers age, the relative number will, of course, increase: playing a guessing game as to whether any of us will be personally affected is not a smart move.

The good news is that the incompetency hand is a much better hand to play if you plan in advance. With that in mind, Part 1 of the book covers the mistakes you will want to avoid in planning for a time of possible mental incompetency in your life.

In this first mistake, let's cover some basic principles and set out the shorthand terminology we'll use for ease of reading.

basic principles to know and keep in mind

1. Planning ahead and preparing the required documentation for a possible time of incompetency does not mean that you will lose control now against your wishes. In fact, with health care delegation, the delegation *cannot* come into effect unless and until it is determined that you are incapable of making the required decisions on your own. Our legal system is (thankfully) based on the notion that people should be free to make their own decisions as long as they wish to and are able to do so.

2. The reluctance of the law to interfere with the decision-making ability of a person and the recognition that personal care decisions are different from property or financial decisions have resulted in legislation across Canada, which in most, although not all, provinces sets out separate processes and documents for the two types of decisions: those decisions that are personal in nature—like health, grooming and diet—and those that affect property and financial matters.

3. For simplicity throughout the book, we use the term *power of attorney* to mean a document that is valid in your province for the appointment of a delegated decision maker for your financial affairs. And no, your attorney doesn't need a law degree: the word *attorney* in this term means *agent* rather than *lawyer*.

4. Also for simplicity, we will use the term *personal directive* to mean a document that is valid in your province for the appointment of a delegated decision maker who will make all the decisions about your health

and personal care, such as where to live, diet, medications, medical treatments and so on.

5. A power of attorney can come into effect as soon as it is signed, if you want, and continue for whatever time period you like. If you are going to Europe and want to sell your house while travelling, you may sign a power of attorney appointing an attorney that is effective for, say, two weeks. Alternatively, and more commonly, a power of attorney can either become effective when it is signed and continue past the occurrence of mental incompetency until the date of death or it can become effective later (maybe when two physicians declare in writing that mental incompetency has occurred) and continue until the date of death. (Deciding which way to go will be part of the discussions you have with your lawyer. The document you sign will then reflect your wishes.)

No matter what you decide to do in your power of attorney and personal directive, if the day comes that you do indeed need some decisions made for you, it may be comforting to know that our laws reflect the belief that a person's decision-making ability is not a simple thing to assess. Comparing the decisions that we make every day for ourselves across a range of topics is not comparing "apples to apples": it is more challenging for a surgeon to carry out open heart surgery than to decide which birthday cake to make for her child. This lifelong reality is taken into consideration when a person's mental abilities begin to diminish. For example, 85-year-old Mary may no longer interact effectively with her investment advisor, but she may certainly be capable of deciding what she wants to wear when she goes out to dinner and what to order once she gets there.

As the next few chapters indicate, it is not as difficult to plan for the possibility of incompetency in your future as you may imagine; instead, it is an aspect of your estate planning that you can think about and plan for one step at a time.

points to take away

▶ Right now in our North American society, we are really not comfortable with talking about being incompetent. We would prefer to die peacefully in our sleep—or keel over while hitting a hole in one!

▶ The benefits to planning ahead for mental incompetency outweigh the difficulty of the process: legislation on the subject in most provinces is designed with simplicity in mind.

▶ Two types of advance planning need to be covered: one for property-related decisions and one for personal care decision making.

OKAY, SO LET'S SAY I'M ALIVE

 MISTAKE #2

Not knowing how to plan in advance for possible incompetency

REALLY, THE MISTAKE we're talking about here is simply mentally blocking out the task of planning ahead for incompetency because (a) it is not at all fun to think about being dependent on anyone; and (b) the terms we introduced in Mistake #1 like *power of attorney* and *personal directive* sound unfamiliar and daunting.

Luckily, once you have done the *thinking* about what you would want to happen if you became incompetent, the actual *doing* with the assistance of your lawyer is relatively straightforward. As the provinces have developed and updated the relevant legislation over the years, they have been guided by the suggestions of practising lawyers and judges and have tried to make this area of the law as user-friendly as possible.

financial matters

The only person who can delegate your decision-making authority over your property and your money is *you,* and you do this via the document we introduced in Mistake #1, a power of attorney. (One lawyer we interviewed mentioned that it bothers her when people say, "I am the power of attorney for my dad" when in fact the correct reference is, "I am the attorney for my dad, under a power of attorney," since a power of attorney is merely a document and the *attorney* is the person named in it. But we digress . . .)

If you don't sign a power of attorney and you do one day need someone to make financial and property decisions for you, all is not lost but the solution comes at a price. Someone in your inner circle of loved ones will need to make a court application and then the court will appoint a delegated decision maker over your property and finances. So the "price tag" includes the extra cost, confusion, and time and effort involved in any type of court application.

An additional frustration with this solution is that the purpose of the court application is to do what *could have been done in advance by you* when you were competent: name a trusted person or persons to look after your financial affairs.

The court-appointed person may not be the person you would have chosen on your own. For example, it may end up being your son, Bert, who lives close by you, but if you had your druthers, your daughter, Susan, would be a better choice. If you had only turned your mind to it when you were able to decide this matter for yourself, you could have chosen her instead. In the worst-case scenario for a court application, Bert and Susan both want the job and are pitted against each other before the period of attorneyship even starts. Or maybe neither wants the role. In this case if you had talked to them about it yourself, you could have addressed the situation by asking your nephew, Joe, to be your attorney.

personal care and medical decisions

When talking about the delegation of personal and health care decisions, if you have not planned ahead and done a personal directive, provincial legislation sets out the people, in descending order of priority, who have the authority to be appointed by a court to make such decisions on your behalf. As in the case of a court application to appoint a decision maker for financial matters, the appointment by the court of a decision maker on health and personal care decisions is a "coulda, woulda, shoulda been avoided" situation that comes at the price of extra time and expense.

If the situation is a medical emergency, there really can be a problem. If there is no personal directive in place and no time for a court application to appoint one or two people as the decisions makers, the presiding physicians may need to consult a number of people who are all in the same category. For example, let's say the doctors need to know if risky bypass surgery should proceed and they need to have that decision made by the category of people with the highest priority to make such decisions. Let's also say that in this example the closest relatives are the adult children. If there are five children who don't get along, they can be feuding in the hospital waiting room for quite some time while the physicians await their decision.

If you think emotional disputes in hospital waiting areas only happen on the Jerry Springer show and never in Canada, hold on a minute—over his many years as a geriatrician, Dr. Michael Gordon, currently the Medical Program Director for Palliative Care at the Baycrest Geriatric Health Care System and one of Canada's best known figures in geriatric medicine, has seen and heard it all from families, some good, and some frankly pretty sad.

In Dr. Gordon's experience, cases do arise where the kids of an incompetent person just can't get it together to make a decision. Often, when they are told that the next step will be for the hospital to ask the appropriate authority in the provincial government to make a decision, they are galvanized to sort it out before that becomes necessary.

Nevertheless extreme situations do occur, where authorities in the province are indeed asked to make an important medical decision and they will do just that, as authorized and directed by law. After this has happened, the family can try to re-assert its position as decision maker through further court applications or dispute resolution, but certainly some valuable time and family dignity will be lost.

points to take away

▶ Provincial legislation directs how residents of the province can plan in advance for an alternate decision maker for financial matters by way of a power of attorney, and in matters related to personal care and medical decisions by way of a personal directive. (As we noted in Mistake #1, the terminology used and the specifics of the legislation vary across Canada.)

▶ If you choose not to plan ahead for a time of possible incompetency, you will *not* be left high and dry, but the required court process to appoint one or more decisions makers will take time and money.

▶ There is also the possibility that a court application will involve needless uncertainty and conflict among your family and close friends, and the chance that someone will be appointed who you would not have personally selected as your decision maker.

JUST GIVE ME CHERRY GARCIA ICE CREAM

MISTAKE #3

Failing to leave a road map for making your personal care decisions and not communicating clearly with your chosen substitute decision maker

SOME ESTATE-PLANNING MISTAKES cost money, some mistakes break hearts. This mistake is in the latter group because not talking about how you think and feel about personal care and health care can leave your loved ones distraught and guilt-ridden.

People glibly say things like, "My kids know they should put me in a home when the day comes," but we wonder, *Have you really had that conversation? Have you written that down in a personal directive?* It is one thing to think we know what our dear mother would want to happen—and quite another to see it in writing. Anyone named as a substitute decision maker in a personal directive is often grateful to see any type of specific written directions to guide his decision and ease his mind when the most challenging ones need to be made.

In Mistakes #1 and #2, we took a bird's-eye view of how to look ahead and plan for a future time when we may not be able to make our own decisions. If that discussion wasn't quite fun enough, we are now taking a closer look at just one of the two types of advance planning: those decisions that are personal in nature.

Think of personal care decisions in two quite separate camps:

- decisions like where to live and what to wear and eat; and

- arguably the scarier decisions about medical treatments when you are incapacitated and not able to absorb the doctors' explanations, weigh the pros and cons, and make up your own mind about what to do.

In this mistake, we are focusing on personal care decisions in the first category—the details of our life when we can't make decisions all on our own, but when we still enjoy aspects of life, even if it is a different life than the one we once lived.

In Mistake #4, we'll talk about delegating medical and end-of-life decision making.

Contemplating not being able to make all of our own decisions—where to live and what to wear—or even having reduced decision-making abilities in any part of our day-to-day life is not fun. You might go so far as to say that they are "Thoughts to Avoid Thinking." And yet, if we choose to, we can map out a decent plan for any eventuality.

Perhaps the most important aspect of personal directive law is the ability in many provinces to name a substitute decision maker to make personal care and health care decisions on our behalf when we cannot make these decisions for ourselves. Who we choose is a crucial selection because it just isn't possible to guess at even the *types* of issues that may come up for our chosen decision maker to decide some day.

It's worth noting here that the substitute decision maker's job is to make decisions, not necessarily carry out all the caregiving himself or herself. These roles—decision making and caregiving—can get confused in people's minds because often the son or daughter chosen to make decisions ends up shouldering some of the actual "implementation" too. For example, he or she may buy clothes for Mom or chauffeur her to medical appointments. But keep in mind that the substitute decision maker named in a personal directive is first and foremost the decision maker.

choosing a substitute decision maker for personal care and health decisions

We've all had the experience of going to buy something, book a trip, select a pet, confident that we knew what we wanted, only to select something completely different once all of the factors were explained to us by a knowledgeable person. Who knew that a Maltese barks a lot? The next thing you know you are bringing home a Shih Tzu.

There's new knowledge in the world every day on every topic, so it only makes sense that the person you name as your substitute decision maker must be someone who will use the same decision-making process as you do: a way of listening to the experts, digesting the facts and making a decision that would be in line with your own approach.

How many people to name in your personal directive? One person whom you trust completely will do just fine, but perhaps you have two people in your life who would likely feel more comfortable working together. This will work out well as long as you know that they will work as a team, ideally with the kind of working relationship that permits either of them to act independently if the other one is unavailable. The last thing you would want is for one of them to order a new blood-sugar home monitor only to have the other return from vacation to start questioning the manufacturer!

Do not be tempted to name all of your children as your substitute decision maker for personal and health care matters—you will hear this message throughout the book—competent people don't need others to hold their hands, and naming all your children because you love them all equally? *Just don't do it:* it is a recipe for friction and delayed decisions.

communication is essential

Now that we have browbeaten you with the absolute need to choose the right person whom you trust, admire and respect—okay, okay, they don't need to be Mother Teresa!—what directions do you need to give them?

Since there are two ways to communicate in life—in writing and verbally—in the case of your advance planning in the area of personal care, consider using both methods of conveying your thoughts, and using them wisely. In thinking ahead to a time when you could have Alzheimer's disease or a related dementia, or could be otherwise unable to make personal care decisions for yourself, ask yourself whether there are specific grooming, diet or other personal care directions that would be important for you, to preserve your dignity.

It's likely appropriate to measure the time you spend getting very specific on these points in your personal directive against your age and stage of life and your state of health, but remember, at any point in our life, tragedy can occur with the result that someone else has to make personal care decisions on our behalf. It is for this reason that, in addition to naming the right person, you will want to be sure that any deeply held personal care wishes are known to him or her. (See what we meant by "Thoughts to Avoid Thinking"?!)

points to take away

▶ You have the opportunity to leave clear directions about what you want to happen, medically speaking and in terms of your personal care, if you choose to do so.

▶ The most important decision is the selection of the substitute decision maker whom you name to make decisions when you cannot: you can't guess at the situations that may arise, or the relevant factors that will need to be considered, so you need to pick the right person.

▶ You should not underestimate the work involved in being a decision maker under a personal directive: The decisions that need to be made can come fast and furious, often with little time for contemplation. Select a person who can handle several things coming at him or her at once and who can keep his or her emotions in check when appropriate.

▶ Use the advance planning process as a time to communicate your wishes to the person named in the personal directive and also by having one or more conversations with that person—ideally on an ongoing basis—about your heartfelt values and wishes when it comes to your personal care.

▶ Remember to update a personal directive regularly. Every three to five years, it is wise to review the document and the named substitute decision maker to see if the directive still makes sense and fits with your current age, health and family situation.

AFTER THE ICE CREAM, I WANT EVERY HEROIC MEASURE KNOWN TO SCIENCE!

MISTAKE #4

Avoiding the difficult decisions and discussions involved with planning for end-of-life medical care

THE MISTAKE HERE is not talking with your loved ones about the touchy topic of how you want to die—or perhaps a better way to put it is how you *don't* want to die. In our interview with Dr. Michael Gordon, Medical Program Director for Palliative Care at the Baycrest Geriatric Health Care System, we heard about a man named George who requested that his elderly mother receive a feeding tube, which, in the opinion of her attending physicians, would need to be kept in place for the rest of her life, with no reasonable hope that she would ever recover from her state of mental and physical incapacity.

The personal directive that had been prepared several years earlier by George's mother was well written and clear, stating that she did not want life-supporting treatment if there was no reasonable hope of returning to a quality of life remotely similar to what she had enjoyed during her life.

George's response to the attending physicians was that the wording was "not what she wanted." *Really?* Had his mother signed a document that clearly said one thing when she meant another? Who knows, but the situation underscores the importance of:

a. preparing a personal directive that clearly states what you want or don't want in terms of end-of-life care and the related quality of life you desire; and

b. talking over what the document means with your loved ones (including the one or two people who are named as your substitute decision maker) and perhaps your physician, to prevent any possibility of the named decision maker not understanding how to make the decisions that may be asked of him or her.

Planning and talking about your personal directive can be difficult, especially when it comes to the medical treatment that you want to receive at the end of your life, but the authority that you place in the decision maker named in the document is significant. Decisions can be asked of that person that will require soul-searching and later some second-guessing if the personal directive is vague or ambiguous.

Phrases such as "heroic measures," "dying with dignity" and even "life support" have little or no meaning to the medical community. According to our interviews, life support measures can be very benign such that directions, even for the elderly or very ill, need to focus on the quality of life desired rather than a blanket prohibition of "life support." At cocktail parties among good friends in the prime of our lives, we say things like, "I've told Archie that I don't ever want to be on life support. Just pull the plug! That's what I want!" Well, as we learned by speaking with Dr. Gordon, it is not quite that easy in real life; we are placed on "life support" anytime we have a general anesthesia for even a relatively minor procedure and we surely don't expect our spouse to "pull the plug" when we are having our ruptured appendix removed.

Dr. Gordon gives the example of cardiac bypass surgery as being a procedure that many years ago may have been considered "heroic." Today, however, a cardiac stent can be inserted on an outpatient basis after the patient has been administered a regional anesthesia. Is this a heroic measure you would decline if you needed it? Uh, not so much.

While writing the book, we also heard about a woman named Gwen whose husband John (age 88) became critically ill with pneumonia. The doctors said that they could try one more thing to save John: They could place him on a ventilator. From their discussions and the terms of John's personal directive, Gwen knew that her husband did not want to be kept alive by so-called artificial means, but she felt that in the doctors' opinions, John had a chance of possibly recovering from the pneumonia. Based on their previous discussions, Gwen believed that John would have opted for a reasonable opportunity to recover and enjoy more time, with a good quality of life.

Fortunately, John recovered nicely and was able to enjoy another year of life before passing away from a massive heart attack. The dilemma faced by Gwen illustrates that the decisions asked of a substitute decision maker are not always black and white. It can be very difficult for a loved one who is the responsible decision maker to balance the goals of benefiting from the advances of medical science, on one hand, and ensuring that the person's end-of-life is congruent with how he or she lived the rest of life. It is not easy stuff! In our view, you probably cannot *over*-communicate what you would want to happen in a variety of situations.

In actually going through the process of preparing your personal directive with your lawyer, you need to first think about your beliefs and values in the area of life-and-death decisions. If you have crystal-clear views on treatments and medical procedures, then it is wise to select a substitute decision maker who shares your views. As much as we would like to think that our vegan cousin's trip to the grocery store before the barbecue can include picking up a couple of nice, thick steaks, we might all end up with tofu burgers.

Then, when you turn your mind to the types of situations that may arise in your life, a few points to keep top of mind are:

- You will likely not be able to plan ahead for every possible medical scenario that may come up in your life.

- Even if you could plan ahead in that way, the medical options available even a week from now may be different than the options available to you today.

- Vague or euphemistic language is not helpful and in most cases leads to further questions.

- Your personal directive is intended to, first, *appoint*, and, second, to *guide and assist* your named substitute decision maker. A personal directive is NOT intended to guide and assist the attending physicians, so aim for clear, articulate statements of your desired quality of life and avoid flowery language as you attempt to describe treatment options that you do or do not want.

points to take away

▶ Think carefully about your values in the area of medical and end-of-life decisions.

▶ Appoint a substitute decision maker in your personal directive who makes decisions in the same way that you do and who ideally shares your values, recognizing that it is impossible to know what decisions may be asked of him or her in the future.

▶ Avoid using vague or euphemistic wording in your personal directive. Focus on descriptions of the quality of life you wish to enjoy and what quality of life would be undesirable for you, rather than on naming the treatments or supports that you would or wouldn't want—the types of treatments and supports can change over time or be appropriate in some circumstances that you can't foresee.

▶ Talk to your substitute decision maker about the contents of your personal directive, discussing some examples and how you would envision your directive being interpreted in these different situations.

HEY, HEY, HEY, HAVE I GOT A JOB FOR YOU!

MISTAKE #5

Glossing over the practical aspects of appointing another person to make financial decisions for you

THE MISTAKE WE WILL LOOK AT in this chapter is the idea that "one size fits all" when providing for the possible delegation of financial decision making. If we were in university, someone stepping into our shoes, financially speaking, would likely just have bills to pay and we would probably have no one financially dependent on us quite yet. By the time we reach our senior years, we may have become an avid and generous patron of the opera and be supporting our widowed brother who lives with us. Thinking about what our power of attorney could and should cover in each of these situations is like contemplating entirely separate jobs.

The way to deal with this evolution of your financial situation is to review and reconsider your approach with each stage of life. In fact it makes sense to address the possible delegation of your financial management in different ways as you go through life. You can do this in a way that is both legally sound and makes sense from a practical perspective:

1. Once you reach the legal age in your province to do a power of attorney, just do it. Appoint a person you trust completely—or maybe two

persons acting together or separately—and at least one alternate. And when thinking about who you most want to appoint, it's a fallacy to think that you should only appoint people who live close by. Sure, it can be more complicated, legally and practically, to have someone appointed who is a plane trip away, but especially in this day and age of email, phones, videoconferences and so on, the best person is the best choice, wherever he or she lives.

2. Make sure you think about the start date for your power of attorney. Will it be legally effective from the first day you sign it and simply held by a trusted person who knows your wishes about when it should be released for use? Or will there be a triggering mechanism in the document so that it becomes legally effective on a certain occurrence, such as one or two physicians stating in writing that you are unable to make financial decisions?

3. As you get older, think about ways to do a gradual transition of your financial decision making. Many older people are quite capable of paying the bills and talking to their portfolio manager, but at a certain age, they decide they are bored with trundling downtown for the meetings and would rather frolic longer in Arizona. So they get their kids involved gradually, which is a practical way to hand over some of the reins and keep an eye on things at the same time.

4. Similarly, if you receive a medical diagnosis at any age or stage indicating that your cognitive ability may be diminishing in the relatively near future, you can plan a gradual transition of your financial decision making at a pace that works for you and your family.

5. Continue to update your power of attorney so that throughout your life it reflects your situation accurately and thoroughly.

6. If your financial affairs are fairly complex and extensive, at age 65, you should speak with your advisor about setting up a "joint partner" or "alter ego" trust. Most often used because of their advantages in the overall estate plan, these trusts set up before death can be a powerful alternative to a power of attorney.

If you take any of these paths, keep your head up and your eyes open—do nothing by rote! Ask yourself each time you turn your mind to this aspect of your planning whether you are just going through the motions or whether you are really thinking about what would happen to your affairs if you pass out on the treadmill tomorrow and don't wake up for a while. Sometimes people assume that things will carry on in the same way if they become incompetent: they assume someone will be able to access their accounts, pay their bills and so on. But even our spouse can't step into our financial shoes unless we have given him or her that legal authority, so it is very important not to make any assumptions.

Think about:

- Your young children. Consider details like who you want to care for them, whether that guardian should be compensated, how and where the kids would live, and how your accounts and other assets would be accessed for your children's care. No one quite knows the details of your life like you do so think about how your assets will be accessed for the care and maintenance of your children if you become unable to carry out the financial management yourself.

- People you are assisting who are not dependents but whom you would still want to benefit if you become incompetent. If you want the monthly payments to your spendthrift but endearing brother to continue, provide this direction, but with the caveat that there always be sufficient income to look after you and your dependents.

- Adult children and grandchildren you are assisting. This category warrants extra attention. If, over the years, you have made a practice of helping out your children and grandchildren when they are in a pinch, how do you want this handled if you become incompetent? This scenario, a common one, can create a touchy family issue, especially if your intention is to name one of them as your substitute decision maker in your power of attorney. Keep in mind that it is one thing to get gifts from Mom or Dad and quite another to receive them from a sibling under Mom or Dad's power of attorney. If you want your adult kids to receive your ongoing support, consider finding ways to look after this in a more permanent way, such as an annuity or a trust set up for them while you are still competent. There will be legal and tax implications to check out before you do this, but you may avoid the possibility of uncomfortable family dynamics.

- Sporadic or annual gifts that you make to people or charities that are important to you. Specify an appropriate range: while you may want these payments to continue, you perhaps don't envision your $50 donations to a few favourite charities "blossoming" to $5,000 Platinum Sponsorships. Or maybe you do! Be clear.

- In all of the above cases, the essential point to bear in mind is that if you do not clearly state what you want done after you are incompetent, your substitute decision maker is legally unable to do anything with your money *other than use it to benefit you*—which is as it should be. So if you want any of your assets to be shared with other people in any way, then you need to clarify that in the power of attorney document.

- And last but not at all least, think about yourself and the desired standards of care and accommodation that you want to receive. It may be wise to clearly state in your power of attorney that you want your assets to be used for the highest level of care and accommodation that your assets can support.

points to take away

▶ Take the time to really think about the best candidate for the job of your financial management. Do you trust that person implicitly to always act in your best interest? Unfortunately, fraud perpetrated by the person named under a continuing or enduring power of attorney is all too common . . . more on this in Mistake #7.

▶ The details in delegating financial decision making need to be thought through, making the process a tricky matter. Ironically the power of attorney is a document often planned in a rote fashion.

▶ Visualize being unable to make your own decisions tomorrow morning and ask yourself how that scenario would really play out, in your own life right now. Think about your children and their needs right now—maybe they still turn to you for financial help even if they are adults. And consider all the other people and situations in your life that would be affected from a financial perspective if you became incompetent tomorrow.

GOOD HELP AIN'T CHEAP

MISTAKE #6

Forgetting about compensation for the people you appoint to act on your behalf if you become incompetent

IT'S A MISTAKE TO EVER ASSUME that if you ask someone, even an adult child, to do something for you, that he or she will do it for free. Saying this makes us sounds very harsh indeed, but we'd rather you thought less of us and avoided a mistake than the other way around. A lawyer who reviewed this chapter said, "People always say, 'Not my kids, my kids won't expect to be paid.' But sometimes they do, and more often than you would think."

There's no way to sugar-coat it: there's a whole lot of fighting about if, when and how to pay people appointed under powers of attorney and personal directives (remember that terminology varies across the country). Estate lawyers call it a minefield and there is a raft of Canadian court cases around compensation for the people asked to take on these roles.

Compensation for a substitute decision maker in the area of health and personal care matters is a particularly tricky area. There's no doubt that often these roles are extremely time consuming and challenging. Nevertheless, unlike the guidelines found in some provinces and court cases about paying a person appointed to make *financial and property-related* decisions on behalf of someone else, people who look after the *personal and health-care* decision making typically find claiming payment an uphill battle.

Other than being reimbursed for their reasonable costs of carrying out the role such as mileage and parking costs when they meet with attending physicians, the role is not typically viewed by the law as subject to a payment schedule. However, that comment doesn't mean you shouldn't consider stipulating a compensation amount in your personal directive. If you feel that the job is worth paying for—and it likely is—you ought to specifically state that in the document. (If the person is your spouse, you are likely good to skip this step!)

If you decide to go that route, discuss with your lawyer the various compensation options for the person named in your personal directive. You could consider allowing the person named in your personal directive to claim an hourly fee or to receive a certain lump sum amount each year in which he or she is acting as your substitute decision maker for personal and health care matters.

The rest of Mistake #6 now focuses on compensating the person appointed in a power of attorney to make property-related and financial decisions, a job that the law in many provinces *does* contemplate as compensable. And as we said at the outset of this mistake, there is a lot of acrimony over the "how much, when and what for" of this compensation.

Why? Well, the reasons leading up to any bitter fight are often multilayered and hard to sort out, but some of the recurring themes seem to be:

- The people making powers of attorney don't think about compensating the person named in it to act.

- If they do think about it, and the person named is a family member, they assume it will be done as an act of familial love, not requiring payment.

- Everyone, both the people doing the naming and the people accepting the appointments, underestimate the work that can be involved, not to mention the tap dance skills required if the substitute decision maker is one of the family and the rest of the family have their own opinions and are ready and willing to share them.

Another part of the problem is the uncertainty about if or when we will ever need a substitute decision maker to make property or financial decisions for us. So it is very hard to properly plan what exactly will need to be done, who the players will be and what issues will come up.

In Mistake #5, we talked about the subtle complexities that tend to be woven into all of our financial lives: money coming from here, gifts going there, donations to that charity and not the other one, this grandchild's special tutor we pay for. It is into this spiderweb that our chosen decision maker steps if and when we are not able to make financial decisions for ourselves.

As well, if incompetency visits us through some form of Alzheimer's or a related dementia, there is sometimes a "grey period" when the person named in the document is helping us out extensively but not really acting as the full-blown, in-charge decision maker quite yet. In later seeking to be paid for all of the work, that individual may believe that the introductory time period of assisting and helping out should be included.

So what to do about all of this? If you decide to name a professional substitute decision maker, meaning that a trust company is appointed in your power of attorney, then in most cases, an employee of the trust company will review with you the compensation that they will charge if and when they act, so you will have a clear picture.

In Jean's years in the trust industry, she observed that even though people may have been initially taken aback by a frank discussion about future fees for future work, they quickly realized the certainty that the discussion provided to them. If and when the trust officers are actually called upon to act as the client's decision maker on financial and property matters (i.e., if the client becomes incompetent), having the compensation formula nailed down in advance goes a long way to creating an effective, amicable situation for everyone.

But let's say you are appointing your substitute decision maker from within your close circle of family and friends: what to do about compensation in that case? You could consider taking a leaf from the trust companies' book and deal with compensation in the document in a clear, thoughtful manner.

Under this approach, you would be wise to ask yourself:

- What is your best estimate as to the complexity of your situation?

- If you think about the work on an annual basis, what amount of time and skill will be required each year? What other work, hobbies or activities will the person named in your power of attorney need to give up or marginalize to carry out the work involved in looking after *your* affairs?

- Can you get some assistance with this issue of compensation? Either your lawyer or your accountant, or both of them, may be able to provide you with guidance as to a method to calculate reasonable compensation for this important role.

- How complicated is your situation? Relevant factors will include your stage of life, your net worth, the types of assets you have and the types of activities and businesses you are involved in. All of these factors can and will change over time, but your current situation provides a starting point for thinking about the kind of work that a substitute decision maker may be required to do some day.

Your other options are to let your document be silent on the issue of compensation or to specifically exclude the possibility of a claim for compensation. If you are leaning in this direction, you likely have excellent reasons for doing so. When appointing a child, for instance, it's hard to imagine that the task would ever be greater than all that you have given him or her over the years as a loving parent.

But times and people change, and when your child is actually acting as decision maker at a time when you are not mentally competent, the situation may be more difficult than you expect. New people may have joined the family (in-laws and outlaws!) or you could be mentally incompetent for a long time, requiring the power of attorney to be in effect for many years before your death. Trust and estate professionals we spoke with also reminded us that family dynamics can change dramatically when the mother or father becomes incompetent; as a thriving, active player in the family circle, you may be the key to everyone functioning together effectively. If you become seriously ill or incompetent, those dynamics may change for the worse.

A better approach than silence or excluding payment may be to think about what the role is worth to you, talk to your advisors and, best of all, talk to the person or people that you want to name:

- talk to them about the nuances that you see in your affairs and how you have addressed them in the document;

- talk to them about what exactly you see them doing for you, if you are incompetent; and

- talk to them about compensation and how you believe that you get what you pay for in life.

In an ideal world, you would also speak with the rest of the family that your chosen substitute decision maker will be working with: there is little doubt that more communication in estate planning helps families feel secure about the future.

Occasionally corporate jargon contains a useful phrase; one such term is *managing expectations*. The best relationships and situations happen when everyone's thoughts and expectations are out in the open. When preparing your personal directive and power of attorney keep the manage-expectations mantra in mind: be clear on your expectations and try to understand the expectations of those who will be affected in a financial way by your incompetency, *including* the person you are asking to do all the work. Now is not the time to bury your head in the sand and hope that everyone in the family plays well together; there's a lot of legal wrangling, past and present, indicating that approach doesn't work.

points to take away

▶ The issue of paying the people named under a power of attorney is a hotbed for disputes.

▶ Trust companies deal with the issue head on by discussing their compensation at the time they are appointed and often setting out what and how they will be paid in an attachment to the power of attorney document.

▶ Even if you are not naming a trust company to act as your substitute decision maker in financial matters, you can consider the same approach to planning for compensation: reviewing the type of work that would likely be required and seeking advice from your professional advisors.

▶ You should also think about talking openly with your loved ones about your respective expectations if you should ever become unable to handle your affairs.

THERE GO THE DANCING DOGS!

MISTAKE #7
Placing too much trust in your delegated financial decision maker

WE'LL ILLUSTRATE THE MISTAKE covered in this chapter with a shocking but true story, one that was well publicized by the media. Brooke Astor, the wealthy New York socialite who died at the age of 105 in 2007, loved her drawing, *Dancing Dogs with Musicians and Bystanders*, a $500,000 piece of art she proudly displayed in her apartment for many years. That is, until the *Dancing Dogs* scampered out the door under the arm of her son and financial caregiver, Anthony Marshall, who apparently decided that he liked dancing dogs too.

The theft of Mrs. Astor's *Dancing Dogs* was one of fourteen charges of which Anthony Marshall was convicted in December 2009. Marshall stole other art, racked up huge personal expenses that he paid from Mrs. Astor's accounts, and conspired with a lawyer to amend Mrs. Astor's will to leave more of her estate to himself and receive a higher executor fee.

Now that an appeal is under way and Mr. Marshall is an elderly man, he may never serve the prison sentence of one to three years. But the five-month trial, with witnesses for the prosecution including Louis Auchincloss, Henry Kissinger and Barbara Walters, raised the shroud from the ugly secret of elder abuse, including the abuse of delegated financial management.

Tempting as it is to think that the "grand theft Astor," as one prosecutor referred to it, doesn't happen in Canada or in families of modest means, the abuse of powers of attorney is a growing topic of concern among a number of people from professions that serve the elderly: social workers, health care providers, lawyers, bankers. When some Canadians are at their most vulnerable, those closest to them are abusing their trust in a variety of ways.

Sometimes the people abusing their appointment under a power of attorney convince themselves that what they are doing is "what Dad would have wanted." For example, they may say, "Dad would have wanted us to have our mortgage paid off by now." Such situations are still abusive: as long as Dad is alive, the money can only be used for his benefit. Other situations are simply out and out fraudulent, where a caregiver, related to the incompetent person or not, freely takes the money or property *because he or she can.*

In 2003, the Alberta Law Reform Institute in Edmonton, Alberta, published a report called *Enduring Powers of Attorney: Safeguards Against Abuse.* Alberta lawyers were surveyed for their anecdotal observations of financial abuses of enduring powers of attorney (the terminology used in that province). They provided a laundry list, which is set out below. It seems eerily like the activities in the Astor case. In reviewing the list below, keep in mind that the term *donor* means the person who appointed the financial agent and the term *attorney* refers to that agent and not to a lawyer.

Alberta lawyers listed these abuses by attorneys under enduring powers of attorney:

- Use of donor's money by attorney for any purpose at all other than the benefit of the donor
- Transfer of donor's money or property to attorney
- Borrowing money on donor's property for attorney
- Prevention of spending of donor's money on donor's maintenance
- Attempting to purchase donor's land below market value
- Family agreement to distribute donor's property while donor was still alive

- Failure to make payments to nursing homes for the maintenance of donor

- Failure to provide money for necessities and comforts

Rather than just wring our hands at the inappropriate use of powers of attorney, you can consider including some safeguards in your advance planning to minimize the chance of this happening to you. *There is, however, no magic bullet.* As the Law Reform Institute paper pointed out, the option of having a supervisory arm of the government to oversee the proper management of each and every power of attorney would be both costly to the taxpayer and highly onerous on the majority of people looking after someone else's affairs in a prudent, honest and ethical manner.

safeguards to consider . . .

1. The Right Person

The best safeguard of all is perhaps the simplest—naming the right person to act on your behalf, or naming two people who you believe will work well together. The principle of "hire well and everything else will fall into place" is one that is followed by successful business people and it fits here too, when talking about choosing a person to look after your affairs if you cannot.

A "doer" who will attend to the management of your money and property with diligence and intelligence, is hard-working, discreet and able to keep your affairs confidential, and is absolutely trustworthy is hallmarks of the person you want. Don't know anybody like that? Consider naming a couple of people to act together, or appointing a trust company (particularly if it is named as one or the sole executor in your will) to either act on its own or with a person from your family or close circle.

2. Clarity In The Document

The law is crystal clear that if Jake is looking after Sally's property, he can only use such property for the sole benefit of Sally, in the absence of stated advance directions from her.

But a common misuse of funds occurs when the attorney under a power of attorney starts to hand out generous gifts and payments from the funds on the pretence that such gifts would have been "what Sally wanted," as we mentioned above. It doesn't matter if the payment or gift is or is not what Sally would have wanted—that becomes irrelevant if and when she becomes incompetent. Upon Sally becoming unable to look after her own affairs, her property can be used only for her care unless she prepared a valid enduring power of attorney allowing specific gifts or payments to be made.

In Mistake #5 we discussed thinking carefully about people who may be affected financially if you become incompetent, for example, siblings whom you are assisting financially even though they are adults. To ensure they continue to be looked after, we said in Mistake #5 that you need to state this. Now, note, however, that another reason for being so clear is that it emphasizes to everyone involved that payments *other than those provided for are not to be made.*

3. A Requirement Of Transparency

Lawyers and governments in various parts of the world have looked at the problem of the abusive use of powers of attorney. One idea that comes up often is to have a person named to be on the sideline, supervising what the substitute decision maker is doing.

The province you live in may have included some aspect of this idea in its legislation, but even if you live in a province where the "monitor" idea is not found in the relevant statute, you could provide in your document that you want your nephew, Bob, to review annually the accounting prepared by your daughter, Carol, who is your named decision maker if you ever become unable to manage your own financial affairs.

Whether your provincial legislation provides a mechanism like this is less important than whether the people named in your document will co-operate. We have laws telling us not to drink and drive, but some people do. Restraining orders can be issued preventing people from being in certain places, but some people under restraining orders will go to those places anyway. You get the idea: while setting up a process for a second review in your power of attorney is something to think about, you also need to be realistic about whether it will work.

The Alberta Law Reform Institute's paper, after discussing several ideas for preventing fraud such as the idea of a supervisory role, puts it this way:

> [Such] requirements would not prevent a dishonest attorney from looting the donor's property and making off with the proceeds. That is something that no legal safeguards that did not involve state administration could do. They would, however, put an attorney on notice that their activities could be scrutinized at any time.

In other words, often just the awareness that someone may be watching, asking questions, even just thinking about what you are doing, may be enough to prevent a substitute decision maker from acting on an idea about an inappropriate use of the money he or she has been asked to safeguard.

4. Advance Communication

Somewhat tied to the discussion above is the suggestion to communicate what you have done to the people directly involved in your power of attorney (the people you have named to act) as well as others who may be affected by your incompetency.

If you are young and healthy, these conversations can be matter of fact and brief. If you are getting on in years and slowing down a little, you perhaps want to spend more time talking to your loved ones about how you see things unfolding, from a financial perspective, as you get older and may be not able to handle things.

Some families seem to operate at two levels: what is said out in the open around the dinner table and then what is said among the adult children and grandchildren, or perhaps among different "factions" of the younger generations. Starting early in your middle years to let your children know that your estate planning is important to you and what you have done will mean that the subject is not taboo and an inappropriate handling of your affairs may be less likely to occur.

points to take away

▶ The fraudulent use of a vulnerable person's money is found in every echelon of society.

▶ There is no governmental watchdog in any part of the world that can effectively protect against such fraud.

▶ Safeguards to prevent your money being used in an inappropriate or even fraudulent manner include:

▷ spending time thinking about your choice of substitute decision maker for financial matters;

▷ perhaps having more than one person named to act together in the role, working together;

▷ naming someone to assume an oversight role; and

▷ communicating early and often among your close circle of friends and family about your plans and intentions.

PART 2

intestacy issues

GIVING AWAY YOUR
STUFF 101

MISTAKE #8

Believing that a will controls the distribution of all of your assets at your death

LET'S BE CLEAR: it is a mistake to die without a will. But it is also a mistake to think that the only document that directs the distribution of your assets when you die *is* a will. To really understand how your estate will be distributed when you die, you need to understand the impact of not only a will but also of joint accounts and beneficiary designations.

So let's take a look at the *three* ways to leave your assets to people after your death:

1. Designations

You can provide for someone by naming him or her as the beneficiary in a life insurance policy, or as the beneficiary on certain types of assets, most notably your registered retirement savings plan or registered retirement income fund (registered plans).

If you like, with appropriate drafting by your lawyer, these types of designations can be made right in your will, confirmed in your will or even changed in your will, but, technically speaking, such designations are not *required* to be put into a will. As long as you have clearly provided the beneficiary's name in the appropriate spot when you arranged for insurance or your registered plans, designations contained right in the plan documents will work, whether or not you also have a will. (It should be noted that if beneficiary designations are made or altered in the will, it is important to discuss with your lawyer the possible ramifications of this on the estate filing taxes or probate fees.)

2. Joint Tenancy With The Right Of Survivorship

You can also transfer all of your interest in some assets through your chosen method of ownership. Specifically, real estate and bank accounts that are held by you and someone else as *joint tenants with a right of survivorship* will automatically become the property of the surviving joint tenant.

This means that no matter whether you have a will or not, assets held in joint tenancy can and will be transferred to the surviving joint tenant. Maybe that's a good thing—or maybe it's a bad thing—it all depends on the end result that you want, but, in any case, it is good to keep the impact of holding property in joint tenancy in mind when thinking about what would happen if you were to die without a will.

(There's an important caveat to mention here about the usual meaning of joint tenancy with right of survivorship, as we've described it above. In recent years, the Supreme Court of Canada has opined that accounts held jointly with an adult child do not automatically by law belong to the surviving child and that before that can happen, some additional evidence is needed to show that the parent really meant his or her adult son or daughter to get the balance in the account upon death. More on this in Mistake #9, but it is a significant point to bear in mind.)

3. A Valid Will

And lastly, of course, you can transfer assets to people through your will. So, after your jointly held assets have moved over into the name of your surviving spouse, for example, and after the beneficiary named in your life insurance policies and registered plans has received those funds (again, often your spouse), if there are still assets in your name, then the distribution of those remaining assets requires a will.

Some examples of this type of asset:

- Any type of bank or investment account in your own name
- Real estate in your name alone

As you can see, a will is essential if your estate-planning intentions cannot be appropriately achieved through beneficiary designations and holding assets in joint tenancy with a right of survivorship. *And*—here's the tricky and very important part—even if you think that your estate-planning goals *can* be achieved by lining up the designations and ownerships, that approach is not always the best way to plan your estate. Some older people who have lost their spouses begin to put their assets in joint names with their children . . . with unfortunate results as we will discuss in Mistake #9.

As well, estate planning done solely through joint designations runs the risk of what people in the estate and trust business call a *joint demise*, meaning both you and your spouse or partner die at the same time in an accident. If you think about it, the person we are most likely to be with if we die an accidental death is our spouse, who is also the person most likely to be our beneficiary and joint account holder.

To sum up, it is a mistake to assume that a will is the only way to transfer your assets after your death. But before you rush into planning your estate through beneficiary designations and joint accounts, take a moment to review the pitfalls of that approach in the mistakes ahead. *In most cases, having a good will in place is extremely important.*

points to take away

▶ There are several ways that assets can be passed on to others after our death, and not all of these methods require a will.

▶ In some cases, the transfer of assets through beneficiary designations and joint ownership is appropriate and simpler than using a will to move those assets.

▶ However, a will is essential for the effective and efficient transfer of other assets and also in situations where beneficiary designations or joint accounts may create more problems than they solve, or where the joint account holder or beneficiary dies at the same time.

An overall caution: it is important to ensure that any intentions you've implemented through your beneficiary designations and the ownership of your assets line up with and match the intentions indicated in your will.

THE ROAD TO HELL
IS PAVED WITH GOOD
INTENTIONS

MISTAKE #9

Avoiding making a will by using beneficiary designations and joint ownership of assets

AS WE STARTED TO DISCUSS in Mistake #8, it is a mistake to rely completely on beneficiary designations and joint accounts as a way to plan your estate. In the context of a committed relationship, holding assets jointly and naming each other as the designated beneficiary of life insurance and registered plans can be a terrific way to easily and effectively transfer assets on the first death to the surviving spouse or partner.

However, this approach to estate planning needs to be used with caution outside of a committed relationship. In other situations, if you use a beneficiary designation or the joint ownership of an asset with any "intentions" tucked away in the back of your mind, you may be creating problems down the road.

insurance designations for minor children

Let's say you are a single parent or perhaps you are married for the second time with children from the first marriage. In either case, you would like to ensure there are funds for your minor children when you die and so you arrange for insurance. When asked to name your beneficiary, you may be tempted to name an adult whom you trust—let's say your brother, Saveng— along with some wording to the effect that Saveng is to hold the money in trust for your kids until your children are adults. It seems nice and simple, but it raises a lot of questions that would come up pretty quickly if you did in fact die while your children were still minors:

- How would you want the money invested?
- Would you want the money available for the children's care and maintenance while they are young?
- Do you want the funds paid out as soon as each child is an adult, or would you prefer that it be held onto by Saveng until they are, say, 25?

You get the picture. Instead of just sketching out the bare bones of a trust that could cause confusion at the time of your death and possibly even litigation in the estate, it would be wiser to either:

a. Name your estate as the beneficiary of the proceeds, with your will then containing trust wording setting out clearly how you want the insurance funds managed for the benefit of your children; or

b. Use an insurance declaration attached to and forming part of your insurance policy to set out the trust terms. A declaration like this would need to be drafted by your lawyer to ensure that it covers all of the important points of the trusts you envision for your children.

joint assets with your child or children

Past the stage of young children? Well, there can still be a pitfall in relying on the no-will-needed approach. Perhaps your spouse has died, you have a couple of grown children, and you recently listened to a talk show on the subject of avoiding probate and how your family can be spared all the hassle of it just by putting everything in joint names.

Next thing you know, you decide to put one of your children onto all of your accounts—and also on the title to your home—as joint tenant with you. Wonderful, you think, when I die everything will be in Sandra's name, there will be no fuss or muss with a will and, of course, Sandra will share all of it equally with her brother. Who needs a will? you ask yourself.

What was the title of this mistake again? "The road to hell is paved with good intentions." Your good intentions could work out perfectly; it would be wrong for us to suggest that there aren't numerous families who have shared everything equally after the last parent died even though all of the assets were held jointly with just one of the children. But who knows what happens after we are gone? Sandra's better judgment could be clouded by financial trouble, or she may have married a ne'er-do-well, as Grandma might say, who influences her unwisely . . . or perhaps she decides that since she did "everything" for you and her little brother in Los Angeles never lifted a darn finger, she should keep the cash. No matter what the reasoning, let the games begin: your plan to minimize hassle and keep things simple has suddenly exploded into the War of the Crocuses.

Again, we don't know what will transpire after our death, and as we mentioned in the last mistake, the courts are now taking the view that when an adult child holds an asset jointly with Mom or Dad, there needs to be some proof beyond the mere ownership to show that the child was supposed to receive the asset as a gift after the parent's death. But the fact that you are reading this book is a pretty good indication that you would prefer to avoid a situation in which your estate becomes involved in a dispute in the first place. For that reason, the wisest approach is to move cautiously about putting assets in joint names with one or more of your adult children: consult your lawyer and weigh the advantages and disadvantages.

points to take away

▶ Holding assets jointly with another person or naming an adult as our beneficiary for life insurance or registered plans is often an effective way to transfer assets, particularly in committed relationships where the named person is the only person to whom we wish to give those assets.

▶ A pitfall with the beneficiary designation approach arises where young children are involved and a well-drafted and comprehensive trust provision would be highly desirable to ensure their interests are fully protected.

▶ The challenge with the joint ownership approach to estate planning when adult children are involved is that your actual intentions may not be carried out.

LET'S CHECK THE CHICKEN COOP!

MISTAKE #10

Leaving behind confusion and heartaches instead of a valid will

IT REALLY IS A BIG MISTAKE to subject your loved ones to the emotional roller coaster that ensues if you don't leave behind a will and one is required. This roller coaster leaves the starting gate the moment that someone thinks, *A will! Did he leave a will?!* and it is a very long ride indeed if no will is ever found.

People die without a will in place for a lot of reasons. They may be an older married couple who think that everything is in joint accounts or covered by reciprocal beneficiary designations and will be looked after that way. Then they die together in a small plane accident, and there is no direction about what to do with the combined estates.

They may be a young, busy couple in the prime of their lives, never thinking that Harry at age 45 could go off to his Tuesday hockey game one evening and never come back, a fatal heart attack ending his life at the rink.

They may be single people—young, middle-aged or elderly—who think they "don't have much," and are not sure whom it should go to anyway; they may not want to face the tough decisions of where to leave their estate or who to ask to be their executor.

For every intestate estate—meaning, an estate where there is not a will, and there should be one—there is another reason why no will was ever prepared.

The irony is that in those estates where no will can be found you often see the situations most crying out for the road map provided by a good estate plan. If the death is early and unexpected, explaining at least in part the procrastination on estate planning, the surviving spouse and family face the double whammy of the emotional impact of the sudden loss, quickly followed by the confusion and even chaos of an intestacy.

the immediate blow

In an intestate estate, sometime between the moment you die and a few days after the funeral, someone who was dear to you will be saying something like: "Was there a will?", "Where is his will?", "Did they do wills?", "I can't believe she never did a will. I'm sure she said she was doing one last year!"

If questions like these are not quickly answered by the appearance of a will, then the worry will begin in earnest, with your loved ones trying to figure out what to do. Maybe they will call a friend of a friend who is a lawyer, maybe they will ask the branch manager at the bank for advice, maybe they will hope the kindly, competent funeral director will have the answers.

Meanwhile, decisions about your burial and funeral must be made without your wishes clearly known, assets in your name alone—such as your house—will need to be looked after, bank accounts in your name will have been frozen until someone is authorized to deal with them, and unpaid bills and questions about what to do and how to do it will pile up with increasing urgency. Because there is no will, no one is in charge yet and no one knows what your wishes would be.

Before too long, if there is any hope that you did in fact leave a will, the search for it will begin:

- A search of your home will be made for either a will or evidence of a safety deposit box.

- Lawyers you may have consulted in the past will be called.

- Trust companies and banks where you were once a client may be contacted about the possibility of either a will you made appointing the trust company, or the existence of a safety deposit box.

- Ads may be placed in law reports and journals asking lawyers to check their wills vaults for your will.
- If your province has some form of wills registry that avenue will also need to be investigated.

medium-term impact

Eventually your distraught family will be advised that without a will, and with assets that need to be transferred, someone in the family must step forward to apply to be the administrator of the estate.

Provincial intestacy law stipulates who has the first priority to apply: usually your surviving spouse, then children if you have adult children, or your parents or siblings if you are single. There may be conflict in the family as to who will act or perhaps no one wants to do the job. Either way, whoever has the job will likely need to hire a lawyer to help them with the court application to make their appointment official.

As one financial planner put it, when there is no will and a will is required, there can be chaos as loved ones try to figure out what needs to be done and by whom:

> It is during this period of confusion where much of the trouble begins to manifest itself. Whether it be family alliances formed, stolen belongings from the deceased person prior to distribution or simply an attempt to gain favour with [the person who may be appointed the administrator], when a will is not drafted it leaves the door open for additional suffering above and beyond that of losing a loved one.

long-term effect

So far we have described confusion, upset, extra time and effort for the appointment of an administrator and extra costs for legal fees. As bad as all that sounds, likely the worst aspect of an intestate estate is really the long-term effect it can have on the people whom the deceased loved.

This long-term effect is the pain caused by a distribution of the deceased's assets in an arbitrary fashion, as we'll discuss in Mistake #11, to people he or she may not have even liked, let alone loved. Conversely, as we'll discuss, the formulaic distribution can, in some cases, completely exclude people who were loved very much by the deceased.

points to take away

▶ Most people would be wise to have a will in place no matter what their circumstances. Often it is the appointment of a guardian for minor children that really causes parents to procrastinate. Try to avoid delaying for this reason because, as we will discuss in Mistake # 12, this particular decision in a will is not necessarily binding anyway. In short, don't let the selection of your children's guardian endlessly delay making a will.

▶ There are many reasons why people die without a will, but whatever the reasons, if a will is needed at your death, confusion will reign if you die intestate (without a will).

▶ The impact of dying without a will includes great uncertainty in the short term, significantly more time and expense for your family and administrator in the medium term, and the possibility of long-term heartbreak and expensive litigation if the distribution of your estate is unacceptable to the people you leave behind.

. . . AND THEN THE REST GOES TO SECOND COUSIN LUCY IN BARCELONA

 MISTAKE #11

Allowing your estate to be distributed according to a cookie-cutter formula

THIS MAY BE THE BIGGEST MISTAKE of all when it comes to dying without a will: letting your assets be distributed according to the legislated formula for intestate estates (i.e., an estate where there is no will and a will is required). One-size-fits-all may work with t-shirts, but it leaves something to be desired when applied to a deceased person's estate.

When Jean was first beginning to concentrate on the practice area of wills and estates, she was mentored by a senior wills lawyer, Don Mackie. Don was a very caring person and he also had a way of making his points in a memorable way.

One of the most important lessons Don felt every new wills lawyer should learn was not to be merely a scribe or an order-taker for clients. The lawyer's role in Don's view was to give the client feedback as to the problems, if any, with their plans, or how their intention as presented could backfire for them, or how to achieve the same thing but in a better way.

Don's advice of tailoring the client's wishes to the will he or she eventually signed was sound because every person and family has special nuances that need to be reflected. Unfortunately, this general principle of estate planning means that a formulaic distribution according to the intestacy legislation is almost always going to be second-rate: *a cookie-cutter approach to estate distribution is not going to work very well, no matter how good the cookie cutter is.*

So what does the provincial intestacy legislation stipulate, generally speaking? It is fairly uniform across Canada, providing that if there is a surviving spouse and no children, after the payment of debts, the estate goes entirely to the spouse. If there are children as well as a surviving spouse, then the legislation specifies the distribution among the spouse and children.

If the deceased did not leave a spouse or children, then the estate goes to his or her parents and if there are no parents, then the estate is divided among the siblings. If a sibling is dead, then his or her children take the sibling's share and so on. Increasingly remote relatives right down to second cousin Lucy in Barcelona may need to be tracked down.

At this point you may very well be nodding your head because you think the above formula sounds like a pretty fair guess as to what a deceased good Canadian would have done with his or her estate had he or she got around to preparing a will. But everyone is unique, everyone's personal and financial affairs are unique, and a distribution that sounds good in theory hits rough ground as soon as it starts to be applied to a variety of deceaseds' estates. Some people who die without a will are young but some are old; some are married but some have simply cohabited with their partner for many years; and some are rich and some are poor. As soon as intestacy legislation starts to be applied to a variety of different lives, all hell can break loose.

It would be hard to set out all of the problems that can arise when an intestate estate is divided up according to the provincial formula, but there are a few really glaring problems that are worth mentioning:

• People may receive an inheritance from your estate whom you really do not like (a spouse from whom you have been separated for many years but never divorced) or you don't even know (cousin Lucy again).

- Intestacy laws in most provinces don't fully recognize common-law spouses. Someone could write a doctoral thesis in law on the various cases and provincial statutes that apply; if you are in a partnership that is not a legal marriage, the key point to take away is that either you or your partner dying without a will may be even more problematic than if you were legally married. It is definitely important that you obtain advice on your estate planning and not assume that when it comes to dying without wills, your relationship will necessarily be on the same footing as a legal marriage.

- Intestacy law as it affects legally married couples can also be confusing— at least one province allows a surviving spouse in an intestacy to choose between (a) taking a share under the intestacy legislation or (b) taking the share of property to which he or she is entitled under family law legislation. Adding to the confusion, a surviving spouse, whether legally married or common law, in most provinces can also make a claim to his or her late spouse's estate for support payments.

- The inclusion of children in the formula sounds good, but it can result in minor children becoming entitled to funds that they are not yet legally entitled to receive. This means that the applicable government body (often called Public Trustee or Public Guardian, but each province has its own term) will manage the money until the children are each adults by law. Two issues here: do you want the money managed in that way while the kids are little, and do you want your children to get the funds as soon as they reach the age of majority? Some teenagers we know (cough, cough) would invest the funds in a new Hummer the day they got the cheque.

If you're a little on the cynical side, you might be thinking that the only people who benefit in these cases are lawyers. But lawyers don't enjoy litigation that arises out of an intestacy. It is hard enough to see a family reeling with a sudden loss, but even worse when an arbitrary division of the estate causes more heartache. Do your part in avoiding that outcome in your own circle by having your will done up and keeping it current at all times.

points to take away

▶ An array of legislation can affect the distribution of an intestate person's estate, creating a formulaic distribution that does not benefit those people whom the deceased really cared about, or carry out his or her desired intentions.

▶ Parents with young children, people in common-law relationships, married couples with significant assets in their own names and individuals who are separated but not divorced—these are just a few of the red-flag situations that can be particularly messy if a death occurs without a will.

▶ Discuss your particular, unique situation with a lawyer and get a will!

MY DIAMOND RING IS GOING WHERE?!

MISTAKE #12

Failing to use estate planning as an opportunity for a thoughtful and careful distribution of your estate, including your personal effects

THIS MISTAKE IS ALL ABOUT the preferences you forfeit if you die without a will, choices that are best made by you but about which you will remain silent by not leaving a will.

These aspects of an intestate estate are:

- funeral and burial wishes
- your wishes about your minor children's guardian
- your directions about who should receive your personal things
- gifts to charities, friends and relatives who are not the main beneficiaries of your estate but to whom you would have liked to leave something

funeral and burial wishes

Estate and trust professionals have mixed opinions on whether to include funeral and burial wishes in wills. For loved ones in the throes of grief after a death, reading the will may not be top of mind until after the burial and by then it will be too late. However, the very fact of preparing a will often starts the discussion about funeral and burial preferences, getting your views out in the open. This discussion usually doesn't happen if people have not gone through the estate-planning process, so at the time of an unexpected death, the family has no direction whatsoever.

minors' guardian

There are two roles in the eyes of the law when it comes to looking after children. On one hand, there is the trusteeship of the funds needed to raise the children, and on the other, there are all the care-related issues that are grouped under the heading of "guardianship": where the children go to school, what they eat, how they are dressed, medical care, and so on.

In an intestate estate where there are young children, with no will in place there is neither a trustee named to administer the minors' inheritances, nor any directions about the preferred guardian. Accordingly provincial law applies to sort out the situation.

In the place of a named *trustee* for the children's trusts, any funds they are entitled to will be held for them by the Public Trustee or Public Guardian (the terminology varies across Canada) of the province where the deceased lived until they reach the age of majority.

To act as the *guardian,* someone will be appointed by the court based on the application put before it by the children's surviving relatives. Again, with no will left behind, the preferences of the deceased parents will remain unknown, although if there is a dispute over the guardianship, chances are good that the parties will each claim that they alone knew the deceased's wishes.

To provide a balanced perspective on this point, when it comes to naming a guardian for your minor children in your will, no matter how emphatically you state who you want to take on that role, when minor children's parents die, the courts always have the final say on the children's guardian. And if you think about it, that makes sense. It is highly likely that the people you want to look after your beloved children are the best people for the job, and the court will agree with your declared choices. However, if the guardian named in a will has taken up an illegal pastime or fallen into the clutches of an addiction . . . well, he or she will not be approved by the court as any minor children's guardian.

With all of that in mind, it is still a shame when parents of young children die without a will, missing the opportunity to say who they would *prefer* to be the guardian for their children.

personal effects

The framed photograph of the original farmstead might not get $5.00 at a garage sale, but watch what happens when there is no will and it's a free-for-all between four brothers who each want it. "Unhappy" doesn't begin to describe how some families feel after the personal possessions of their parents are distributed in the wake of an intestacy.

The distribution of an estate when no will has been left behind is all based on a black-and-white distribution of the *value* since no legislation could ever purport to divide up personal property in a way that made sense. This means that on the face of it, the personal property should all be sold by the administrator (once one is appointed) and the proceeds divided in the formulaic manner driven by the intestacy legislation we discussed in Mistake #11.

However, with the agreement of the beneficiaries entitled to the estate, the administrator may try to carry out a fair distribution of the actual items without selling them. The difficulties of this approach, though, will include: (a) getting that agreement as some of the beneficiaries may just want everything sold and (b) proceeding to split them up in a fair manner. If the beneficiaries believe that the distribution should be based on an assignment of monetary value to each item, some items such as valuable art or jewellery can be appraised, but it will be hard to value those items that are largely sentimental in value.

The personal effects in many intestate estates have been divided up amicably—there are many options for carrying out the process, such as the eldest child of the deceased choosing first and then the next oldest child, and so on in that order until all the effects are distributed. As in so many situations, it will be as "easy as pie" if people want to make it work and unbelievably difficult if sibling rivalries or other emotions are brought along to the task.

gifts to charities, friends and relatives

This is a catch-all category for the people and organizations that you would have included in your will, even in a small way, if you had prepared a will. Even if the overall distribution of your estate according to the intestacy legislation is acceptable, there is no provision in it for the smaller, personal gestures that people so often like to make in a will. The church that you attended for many years, the next door neighbour who mowed the lawn, the godchildren who were important to you . . . these types of gifts, whether you would have made them large or small, won't happen if you die without a will.

People can be amazingly kind and will sometimes carry out on behalf of a deceased person what they know he or she would have wanted, such as gifts to favourite charities or a special piece of china passed on out of the possessions that were received from an estate. But drawing up a will is a more certain and convenient way for everyone to make sure that these little remembrances really happen.

points to take away

▶ A person who does not leave a will misses out on a golden opportunity to specify important personal preferences.

▶ These preferences include a statement about preferred funeral and burial wishes, your preferred guardian for your minor children, how you want your personal effects divided, and miscellaneous gifts of money or items to charities, friends and more remote relatives.

SHARE, SHARE AND SHARE ALIKE . . . SHARING YOUR ESTATE FAR AND WIDE . . .

MISTAKE #13

Overpaying for bonding, taxes and professional fees because you die without a will

HOW WE REACT to the cost of things is very personal: some people really care about not overpaying for anything, while others just care about managing certain types of expenses or watching outlays over a certain dollar amount.

When it comes to the expenses of their estate, some people are rather indifferent it seems, taking the view, "I won't be around anyway, so who really cares?" Your personal perspective will determine how perturbed you'll be at the news that your estate without a will will almost certainly pay more for **bonding**, it may pay more in **taxes**, and will quite likely wind up with a larger bill for **professional fees**. We'll look at each of these costs in turn.

bonding

When there is no will and nobody named by the deceased to carry out the work of the estate, it is a little risky from the law's perspective to simply appoint someone who has stepped forward to be charged with this important task. For this reason, in an intestate estate a bond is required to make sure that the administrator does a good job, protecting both beneficiaries and creditors of the estate. The value of the bond is usually twice the value of the estate. Posting the bond with the court requires either willing individuals with sufficient net worth to step forward and provide evidence that they have net worth to cover the bond, or the administrator must approach a bonding company to provide security paid for by an annual premium similar to a life insurance policy premium. If the administrator has a good credit rating, the cost of the premium may only be hundreds of dollars, but the difficulty, time and aggravation in applying for and obtaining it is often considerable.

The cost of the bond will depend on several factors, including the value of the estate and the kinds of assets in it. This bonding requirement in an intestate estate is in contrast with an estate where there is a will. In that situation, unless none of the executors named in the will are from the province where the deceased lived and where the estate is now resident, the posting of a bond to ensure the executor's proper and ethical administration is not usually required. (Presumably the law takes this approach because the executor was selected by the deceased, so he or she is assumed to be a trustworthy type.)

taxes

An intestate estate does not *always* pay more tax than an estate governed by a will, but it can happen if you leave behind capital property that has increased in value since you acquired it. Examples of capital property are real estate other then your primary home, an investment portfolio not in a registered plan, and shares in a private business. If this type of property has increased in value, capital gains tax may be payable when you die. However, if you leave the property to your surviving spouse, your estate has an opportunity to take advantage of a capital gains tax deferral that is available under the *Income Tax Act*. This deferral allows you to "roll over" your capital property—gains and all—to your surviving spouse, such that the payment of tax on the gains is postponed until he or she later sells the property.

But—*and here is the lost opportunity*—if you die without a will, the distribution under the intestacy legislation may require that some of the estate (including the capital property) goes to the children, forfeiting the capital gains tax deferral, or rollover.

To put it another way, if the applicable intestate distribution does not entitle your surviving spouse to receive all of your capital property, the rollover provision under the *Income Tax Act* is not available on property going to children and—bingo!—taxes are paid at your death rather than deferred.

As tax professors like to quip, taxes deferred are taxes saved.

professional fees

If we were playing a word association game, the word we'd associate most quickly with intestacy would be *uncertainty*. *Who knows* what will happen when a person dies without a will? Even the most experienced estate lawyers in the country couldn't give your family a quick, off-the-cuff description of what exactly will need to be done if you die without a will. "It depends," would be the most common response.

The complexity of the situation and what needs to be done will be determined by many factors, such as:

- how you held your assets (jointly with anyone or not);

- what assets you had;

- whether you were married or in a common-law relationship, or have been married before;

- if you have children, and their ages;

- how much your estate is worth;

- how your family gets along (or not); and

- whether there is an obvious choice to be the administrator that everyone in the family agrees with

Since uncertain times are when we most need to rely on good professionals, dying without a will may very well result in significant fees paid to both a lawyer and an accountant to determine the answers to the above questions (and others) and then put together a plan of action. This will take time; one lawyer we spoke with suggested that an application for the court order in an intestacy is at least twice as long as where there is a will.

If there is also *conflict* in the family, all bets would be off as to (a) the time required to sort it out, and (b) the professional fees to help your loved ones do the sorting.

points to take away

▶ Not everyone worries about the costs in their estate ("I'll be dead anyway!"). However, keep in mind that the extra costs in an estate where there is no will can be high.

▶ A bond will be required in an intestate estate, with the cost determined by the makeup and value of the estate.

▶ Additional tax expense can arise if the deceased would have been entitled to roll capital property over to the surviving spouse but doing so is prevented by a partial distribution to children under the intestacy provisions in the deceased's province.

▶ The most uncertain and therefore most worrisome added cost in an intestate estate is the higher cost for professional advice. It is impossible to know in advance what the legal, accounting, financial planning and investment advisory fees will be to assist your family in sorting out your affairs if you die without a will.

PART 3

will-planning errors

IS THAT SNORING
WE HEAR?

MISTAKE #14
Taking the back seat in your own estate planning

NO ONE PLANS TO SIGN a will that isn't quite right and we certainly aren't suggesting that professionals who assist people in preparing their wills are at fault. But the frequency of not-quite-right provisions and even blatant mistakes in wills makes us realize that it is too easy to fall asleep when we should be most alert.

Every article and book on estate planning starts out by recommending that you consult with your own lawyer and accountant before acting on the ideas in the article or book. We agree with that advice.

And estate and trust professionals steer you away from using a hand-written will or a wills kit.

And we agree with that too: wills are best prepared by professionals and we will spend a few chapters explaining why that is.

But here are some essential points that you really need to remember when you retain a professional to assist you with your wills, as you should:

- No one knows your affairs and your life like you do.

- No one cares about your affairs and your estate planning like you do.

This may sound trite, but you are the "CEO" of your life and your professional advisors work for you, not the other way around. A CEO sets the strategy, provides guidance and makes the final decisions: even though your advisors bring expertise that you do not have, you still have the ultimate responsibility for your will and estate planning and you need to understand every clause of your documents.

- If you climb into the back seat and take a nap while you and your lawyer, accountant or team of professionals are collaborating on your will, it will not be as good as it should and could be.

This concept of taking responsibility for your estate planning is so important that we would like to repeat these points again but that would be annoying, so please just read them over one more time.

Time and again, both grieving relatives and trust professionals have been perplexed—after someone's death—by one or more clauses in the deceased person's will. They may say to themselves: *What was she thinking? How could Uncle Joe have wanted that? Surely that is not what Mom meant to do? It doesn't make sense!*

Well, likely it doesn't make sense and chances are that it did not make sense when the will was signed. But, somehow, some way, the error, big or small, purposeful or just a "miss," made by a sole practitioner or a team of professionals from large firms, slipped through the cracks. Obviously there are some factors at work that we all need to be on guard for.

Consider these scenarios and whether they sound like possible traps for you in your estate-planning process:

- You have put off preparing a will, so once you start, you just want to get it over with and you don't pay too much attention to it.

- You (consciously or not) try to keep an arm's length from the subject matter, which of course is not very pleasant since it concerns your death.

- You are reluctant to ask your advisor to explain terms you don't understand or to discuss complicated paragraphs that you think (hope!) reflect your verbal directions to the advisor, but you are really not sure if they do or not. The fact is, you are afraid you will be embarrassed because the lawyer or the accountant seems very smart and confident and they sure do seem to know their stuff.

- You hesitate to raise certain topics or concerns with either your spouse or your advisor because the area is a sensitive one or very private and you'd rather not get into it.

- Deep down inside you are quite sure that this won't be your last will and you tell yourself that the next time you prepare a will you will pay more attention and address the niggling concerns on your mind.

We could go on, but you get the point. Avoidance thinking helps keep us sane and lets us enjoy life to the fullest: When we are savouring the eight-course tasting menu on Valentine's Day, we aren't thinking about what the scale will say at Jenny Craig the next week. When we kindly volunteer to help out a sick friend, it is good to block out our New Year's resolution to read 52 books in the year because our gift of time will blow the reading resolution for that week.

But will planning is high-stakes stuff, with a lot to lose if we're successful at "faking it." The more we can really sweat the details, and think carefully about the decisions we're making and how they will really play out when we are dead, the better the chance we won't leave our loved ones perplexed and saying, "Huh? Really?!"

In Jean's experience, people who have been diagnosed with a terminal illness tend to focus most carefully on their wills. Sadly, very ill people know they don't have licence to treat the process as an item on the to-do list along with redoing the hardwood floors. They know that this is their last will and they treat the process accordingly.

Think about it.

points to take away

▶ Even with the most talented lawyer to assist you, don't forget who "owns" the will-planning process. Small and large errors, oversights and unnecessary complexities can lead to a will that is less than perfect, creating big problems later.

► Pay attention during the process, put yourself into the shoes of your loved ones after you are gone, and read through your draft will from that perspective. Ask yourself: does every clause make sense? Is it what I want?

► If it is appropriate for you in your family situation, openly discuss all of your concerns and worries with your spouse and family so that your will achieves your sincere intentions.

► Force yourself to ask questions of your advisors—there are really no stupid questions in this complex area of the law.

AND FOR MAKING THOSE DELICIOUS MUFFINS, I LEAVE MY HOUSEKEEPER ONE MILLION DOLLARS ($1,000,000) WITH MY LOVE AND AFFECTION!

MISTAKE #15

Not understanding the importance of mental capacity when preparing a will

WE HAD TO DISCUSS FOR a while how we'd fit this "mistake" in. It felt a little harsh to call preparing a will when incompetent a mistake, since if a person is mentally fit, he or she wouldn't be making the mistake. But we decided to include it as one of the "50 Biggest" in part because the law on testamentary capacity is so darn interesting but also because understanding the required state of mind that is necessary to prepare a valid will is important. Knowing about it may be useful both for your own planning and as you observe the estate planning being done by people you care about who are getting on in years.

After reading even just a few cases on testamentary capacity, it becomes clear that the law itself is fairly straightforward but applying it to each unique situation is invariably challenging for the judge. Perhaps one of the main reasons for this difficulty is that capacity is a moving target, with our mental abilities shifting not only very slowly as we age, but even from day to day or hour to hour. Think about the times when you are sharpest: tasks that felt overwhelming when you were tired or drained can be a snap to complete when you're feeling energetic and "in the mood."

Sarah describes herself as a night owl whereas Jean is a morning person: most people claim to fall into one of these camps. Why do we select these labels for ourselves? Because we feel brightest at our preferred time of day, better able to tackle big jobs or deep thinking.

This subtle daily variation that many people experience throughout life is not wholly different from an elderly or very ill person's good days and bad days, except that on the bad days, perhaps he or she would not meet the test to prepare a valid will—or maybe that person would. In a 2009 Ontario decision that looked at several issues including testamentary capacity, Justice Newbould commented about the mental state of the now-deceased man: "It is not surprising that a man with advanced cancer would tire and repeat himself or exhibit confusion at the end of the day after a family meal."

The judge went on to decide that the man did in fact have the required capacity to prepare a last will. See what we mean? It's complicated.

how it all works

When a person dies and a will is found that is believed to be the person's last will, it is *presumed* to be a valid will, properly signed and made by the person when he or she was mentally competent to prepare a will. This "presumed-valid" will gives immediate authority to the person named in it as the executor to get busy with all that needs to be done. (Terms for the personal representative of a deceased person's estate vary but for the sake of simplicity, throughout the book, we will use the term *executor*).

In some cases, the executor will need to obtain a court order formally appointing him or her so that the deceased's property can be dealt with and eventually distributed according to the terms of the will. Although now a somewhat outdated term, you may hear this process called *getting probate* or *applying for probate*, and we will discuss this process later in the book.

In the majority of estates, the presumption of a will's validity is never questioned, but in some situations, people who feel that the will's contents are inappropriate may make a claim to the executor that the deceased's last will was not valid for some reason, most likely including one of these claims:

- It was not signed properly and therefore is not valid.

- The deceased person did not have testamentary capacity when it was signed and therefore the will is not valid.

- There was someone in the picture at the time the will was being prepared and signed who exerted undue influence. This influence affected the deceased's decision making, and therefore the will is not valid.

Once a claim like this has been launched, the ball volleys back to the executor to "prove" the will: to establish that it really was signed in accordance with the rules for signing a will in that province; to establish that the deceased did indeed have the required capacity; and to dispel the suggestion of anyone unduly influencing the deceased in such a manner as to invalidate the will.

the tests for capacity

As we have hinted above, determining who has the mental capacity to prepare a will and who does not is tricky. The legal tests for the mental capacity to prepare a will cover points such as:

- Did the person doing the will know what he had to give away and to whom he was giving it?

- Did he understand that certain people in his life might feel they had a claim to his estate?

- Did the plan make sense in the overall context of the estate planning that the person had done all his life?

When a suggestion of "undue influence" is added to the mix—as it so often is in these cases—the court needs to assess whether that involvement and influence was sufficient enough to actually strip away or reduce the capacity of the person to prepare a valid will.

To see how undue influence works, imagine an elderly person named Sally. Sally is vulnerable. She does not feel well, she is scared, she is physically and mentally diminished but let's say that she is surrounded by her loving family, who only care about Sally's best interests. It is possible that Sally would still be able to give valid will instructions, at least on certain days and perhaps in the mornings, for example.

However, now imagine a situation in which Sally is alone in a small apartment, without a loving family, and add in a preying, opportunistic person named Harriet, who clearly sees a relationship with Sally as an opportunity to come into some wealth. If without Harriet, Sally will be stranded in her home, but with Harriet, she is able to go to her medical appointments, get groceries and go for a Big Mac once a week, the influence of Harriet over Sally in all matters (including her estate planning) is entirely different than the influence a type like Harriet has over a less vulnerable person. And maybe that influence would therefore be sufficient to negatively affect Sally's testamentary capacity.

It might be useful to pause here and mention that when a court is looking at whether a person had the capacity to prepare a will, it doesn't hold the will up against a raft of standards like tax effectiveness, use of the most trust-savvy planning, or community-mindedness. In fact, in most provinces, testamentary freedom is broad, such that a parent can even exclude his or her adult (non-dependent) children from the will; only a couple of Canadian provinces, such as British Columbia and Nova Scotia, have legislation on will variation allowing a claim by disinherited adult children on the basis of a moral duty.

how does this affect me?

So, you might be wondering what to make of all this. We suspect that if you are reading this book, the chances are good that you have the capacity to sign up a valid will. But there are two situations in which testamentary capacity may be a relevant topic for you:

1. If you intend to do something in your will that may not please everyone, such as disinheriting your second and fourth child, just as an example.

In this situation, you need to run, not walk, to a good wills lawyer to whom you will explain in careful detail exactly what you want to do and then you need to listen to the lawyer's advice as to whether you can do this, and, if so, the best way to increase your odds of avoiding litigation over your estate after your death. *It is absolutely essential that you do this if you live in a province where leaving out an adult child can be challenged; your lawyer will be able to advise you about your province's legislation.* Your lawyer will provide you with the advice and directions that you need, make suggestions about how to achieve your goals (if that is even possible) and what the pros and cons are of your approach. If you are up to it, you could also think about communicating your intentions to the very people who may be upset about them.

2. If you observe a vulnerable person who appears to be doing estate planning that doesn't fit with his or her past approach.

If you find yourself in this situation, once again, you will want to rely on good, proactive counsel to assist you to canvas the options about what you might be able to do. The key here will probably be to encourage Sally to see her own lawyer, separate and apart from Harriet; this won't be easy as these situations are often very complicated, perhaps even including mental or physical abuse. Professional advice is definitely required because in trying to help a vulnerable person, it is a big mistake to attempt new planning behind the scenes. A handwritten will or will kit prepared in a situation such as this will not likely be seen after the person's death as a useful addition to the mess.

points to take away

▶ A will's validity can be challenged if it is not executed (signed and witnessed) properly or there are other problems with adherence, or lack thereof, to the formal requirements of a valid will.

▶ A will can also be found to be invalid if the person who signed it lacked testamentary capacity or was unduly influenced by another person when preparing the will.

▶ Testamentary capacity tests do not aim to ensure that wills are "perfect" or even "wise." The goal is to make sure that people know what they have to give away, who might care about it, who they are benefiting and in what way, and that they understand the overall plan.

▶ The inappropriate or aggressive involvement of someone else in the will-planning process may later be found by a court to constitute "undue influence," which in turn eliminated the deceased person's ability to give instructions for a valid will.

▶ A couple of Canadian provinces do not have unfettered testamentary freedom, meaning that if you live in those provinces it is particularly important to obtain experienced legal advice on any distribution that may be challenged by family members you wish to exclude.

▶ The best strategy to avoid the hardship of litigation over your estate or that of a person you care about is to find and hire a good lawyer, experienced in these issues, to assist you in increasing the likelihood of a positive outcome.

INSERT SECTION A INTO WIDGET B AND POUR IN RUBBER CEMENT

MISTAKE #16

Leaving behind a handwritten or will-kit will instead of retaining professional assistance

THERE ARE TWO WAYS in which a do-it-yourself will can backfire and become a big mistake. The first is when the actual tangible document is incorrectly prepared; the second is if the contents of the document are flawed even though the document itself is prepared and signed according to the law. In either case, your estate can wind up in mediation or litigation, taking much longer and costing much more than if you had just gone through a proper estate-planning process with some good professionals at your side.

But writing about handwritten wills and will-kit wills is maybe like being a registered dietician before bikini season: they must suspect as they drone on about the risks of crash diets that all of their wise advice may go up in smoke the next time their client is in line at the grocery store. It can be game over for sensible eating upon spying a tabloid headline that screams, Chocolate Bar Diet whittles 10 pounds off Jennifer in a week!

So we aren't going into this discussion unaware that the Write-Your-Legal-Will business isn't highly profitable for somebody and we have no doubt that some of you who are reading this book either have such a will or, against our advice, will one day wander into a bookstore and sneak out with the kit, including the CD.

Just don't say we didn't warn you about it.

In our extensive discussions with lawyers who focus on estate litigation and trust officers across Canada, we struck out on finding anyone with positive words about do-it-yourself estate planning. It is not that handwritten wills can't be prepared in most Canadian provinces and it isn't that the kits necessarily contain inaccurate instructions. The problem is that the knowledge to effectively use these will methods is missing because, uh, they are not being filled in by estate lawyers. The average person—no doubt a wizard in his or her own realm of dentistry, heavy-duty mechanics or hockey parenting—is out of his or her element when it comes to directing the disposition of assets after death.

As we said at the outset of this mistake, do-it-yourself will planning can sometimes result in either a flawed document because the will signing formalities are not followed, or a properly signed document but one in which the contents include small ambiguities or big mistakes.

the formalities of the document

There are a couple of approaches for a person attempting to make a will on his or her own: one is to prepare a holograph will (and keep in mind that these are not legal in all provinces) and the other is to prepare a formal will.

What is required in a holograph will in those provinces where they are valid was set out in a 1962 Supreme Court of Canada decision: a valid holograph will must be entirely in the deceased's own handwriting and signed at the end, and it must convey the intention to be a "deliberate, fixed and final expression as to the disposition of the property of the deceased on her death."

In the 1962 case,[1] as in most cases relating to holograph wills, the will left behind did not deal with all of the deceased's property and it did not

---

1. Canada Permanent Trust v. Bowman, [1962] S.C.R. 711.

name an executor. And, most important of all, it took three courts, right up to the Supreme Court of Canada, to reach the final decision that the flawed little document actually meant anything! Although it is unlikely that the Supreme Court of Canada will opine again on holograph wills, even leaving your affairs in such a state that any court is required to look at your hand-drafted will is a sorry waste of time, money and family harmony.

The main requirement for a formal will—that is, one that is typed or otherwise not drafted in the person's own handwriting—is proper witnessing. This involves a careful signing process where three people are all together as the will is signed: the person whose will it is and the two witnesses, neither of whom should be a beneficiary under the will. Proper protocol for signing a will includes each of those three people not only signing the will at the end, but also initialling each page to ensure nothing gets added or changed later. (A lawyer who read this mistake for us wrote in the margin, "It is amazing how many people assume that it is okay for each witness to sign the will at a different time—they don't understand that they all have to be together at the same time!!")

These rules apply to a will-kit will because it is not entirely in the person's own writing: it is either a form with blanks to be filled in, or a CD with the document to be revised on a computer. Because the execution procedure is tricky, formal wills attempted by laypeople are often rendered invalid because the procedure is flawed. Perhaps the person preparing the will thinks that the witnesses are just a "nice-to-have" rather than a "need-to-have" or maybe the witness is a beneficiary (oops!) or maybe the person signs the will on Monday and the next door neighbours act as "witnesses" on Wednesday (oops again!). Unless you are trained in how to prepare a will properly, it is very easy to make a misstep along the way.

the contents of the document

Even if the document itself is prepared according to the law and it is successfully accepted as a valid will, the trouble may just be starting.

Do the contents make sense? Are the will's provisions what the person really meant? Are all of the person's assets actually going to be dealt with by the will when he or she dies, or is the will just a snapshot of the assets owned at the date of the will?

To bring our point to life, let's contrast the self-help approach for wills with what you get when you use a professional.

One thing that they teach in law school that is not helpful in day-to-day life but is pretty useful in estate planning is how to be negative and cynical. Trained this way, good estate lawyers will grill you with questions like, What if she is also dead, then what? What if all your children get divorced? Eventually you may feel like running out of their office screaming, but you'll also end up with a will that addresses every possible outcome.

And sure, some of the scenarios in your will may not happen, but if they do, you'll have a will that works. The alternative is dying with a home-made work of art that includes things like outdated bank account numbers, since it didn't occur to you—not being a negative lawyer and all—that before your death you might get mad at the green bank, move to the blue one, and not have those specific bank accounts any longer.

If that happens, an arsenal of experts in estate litigation and maybe a mediator or a court will need to figure out whether you meant that "any" bank accounts you had when you died were to go to your godson, or did you mean that only those accounts at the green bank, if you still had any, were to go to him?

Hmm, hard to know.

See what we mean? Do-it-yourself will planning is a land mine.

points to take away

▶ In most provinces (always get advice on this point!), the law provides that people can leave a valid will behind that they have prepared on their own. If a will is entirely in a person's own handwriting and signed at the end, it is a holograph will.

▶ If a will is prepared under the auspices of a will kit of any type and therefore includes words that are not in the person's own handwriting, then it will be a formal will and is therefore subject to the formal will-signing procedure.

▶ Either way, any will prepared by a layperson (not a lawyer) may not include everything that it should include, or it may be overly descriptive, which can also cause interpretation problems.

▶ Using a lawyer who is experienced in estate law—and staying alert during the whole process, see Mistake #14!—is the best way to get what you want in your will.

I'LL NEVER LOSE IT
UNDER THE SILVERWARE!

MISTAKE #17

Storing your will incorrectly

THE MISTAKE WE WILL LOOK at in this chapter really amounts to underestimating the value and importance of the original will document. This is because *an original will is a valuable document that is generally presumed to be revoked if it cannot be found at our death.* What with copiers, scanners, computers and the like, today we frequently copy and scan documents, storing the resulting copies in all sorts of electronic and real folders. Often a copy of a document is good enough for a later purpose but an original will is different: there is only one original will and a copy of it just doesn't count for much.

When an original will is missing at the time the person dies, it is presumed by the law to be—don't smirk here—*lost*, unless there's evidence to suggest that the deceased didn't mean to lose it and that its contents (as found in a copy) should still prevail. In other words, the law says that if your original will was last in your possession and cannot be found after your death, you are presumed to have destroyed it with the intention to revoke its contents because they no longer reflect your true wishes.

Now it might seem obvious to you that a lost will was meant to get lost, but just because something is missing doesn't mean we meant it to go missing. Take your favourite brownies recipe that you tuck into the pan that you use for brownies (with its special lid and all). You decide to make brownies and the recipe isn't at hand; months later, after going through every recipe file in the house, you come across the recipe in its crafty hiding place. *Of course*, you say, smacking your forehead!

A case from Nova Scotia considered a situation involving the loss of an original will. The deceased man had worked around the world as a chef, without a fixed base or home where he would logically keep valuable documents. Although his original will could not be found, there was a copy of it. The provisions of the will, as found in this copy, gave his estate to his siblings with whom he was close, and excluded his father from whom he was estranged.

All of the evidence about his lifestyle and his family relationships suggested that the late chef meant the contents of that missing will to still apply. As a result, the court directed that the copy of the will could be admitted to probate, which simply means that the court was accepting the use of the copy in the same way as it would have accepted the original document.

More important than the niceties of the law on this issue, though, is to keep in mind that a court application was required at all. The time, energy and money that go into a court application on a will question can't be overstated—and that is never a good thing. Even if all the people magically come away pleased with the answer, the process itself will have been a financial drain on the estate and an emotional drain on everyone involved with it.

So, where to store a will? Ideally you will think carefully about two documents that need to be stored: the will and the copies, and while you are at it, the same principles of storage and distribution apply to your personal directive and power of attorney.

the original will

The original will should be stored with the lawyer who assisted you with it, or the trust company that you named to be an executor (more on executors later). The advantages of this approach include certainty as to the original will's location, prevention of inadvertent revocation of the will if it cannot be found, and storage of the document in a fireproof vault.

Another alternative, but not as good, is to store the original will in a safety deposit box. If you choose that route, give clear directions to the person named in it as your executor as to where the safety deposit box is and how to access it. *Do not store your original will in your mattress, a filing cabinet, desk drawer, or the like.*

copies

A copy of your will should be stored in a place where it would be readily found on your death: here is where you could consider your filing cabinet or desk drawer.

Make sure to clearly mark on the front page of this copy where the original will is and:

a. the name and phone number of the lawyer who prepared it and, if applicable, the names and phone numbers of the professionals at the trust company appointed in your will as the executor; or

b. the branch, location and phone number of the bank where the safety deposit box is and, if possible, the name and direct phone number of the person at the branch who could most readily assist your executor to retrieve the original will.

What about giving a copy to anyone else? Caught up in the excitement of completing their estate planning, people can get overenthusiastic about sharing their wills. Remember that even though you should approach your will planning as if this is indeed your last and final will, there is always the chance that you will do another one. Particularly if you are "pretty young," a relative term that we'll leave to you to define, you may be wise to hold off actually handing out copies of your will until you are starting to delegate aspects of your financial affairs to your children. At that point, you may want to share a copy of your will with each of them. Until then, hand out your famous brownie recipe and leave it at that.

points to take away

▶ A will is a valuable document and its contents are considered by the law to be revoked if the will itself cannot be found at your death.

▶ However, the contents of the lost will may still be permitted to take effect if a court accepts the evidence presented at a court application that the deceased person intended the lost will to apply. But the most important thing to keep in mind is that a court application should be avoided if at all possible by the proper storage of both the original will and copies.

▶ The original will needs to be placed in the safe storage of a law firm or trust company, or in a safety deposit box.

▶ The copy should be easy to find and have the original will's location clearly written on it.

▶ The essential information that your family and named executor must know when you die is where to find the original will. Later in life you may want to discuss the contents of the will more fully with your family and at that stage, give them a copy to review.

PENNY-WISE AND POUND FOOLISH

MISTAKE #18

Trying to change your will by writing on the original or a copy of the will, or using too many codicils

IT IS AN EASY MISTAKE, THIS ONE: assuming that the breezy informality of modern life can be applied to making changes to our wills. We live in a world where changes are viewed as something to make on the fly via a BlackBerry, and the strict rules about changing wills can be easily forgotten. If the teens in our lives can de-friend people by a keystroke on Facebook, surely we can make a simple little revision to our will?

Uh, the answer is no, we can't. Changes to wills must be made according to the same rules we talked about in Mistake #16 for signing a will in the first place. Done incorrectly, changes attempted by writing on the will itself or even by the use of a separate document can wreak havoc. Your artwork in will amendments may not only fail to make your desired revision but, worse, it could also revoke all or part of the will that you are trying to change.

And here perhaps is the most important point: a court application may be required to figure out what to do with a will revision that you attempted on your own, resulting in significant time and money being spent to

determine whether and how the attempted amendment affects the distribution of your estate.

You may be saying, Look, I will read the rules, I will figure it all out,
I know that I can effectively make some changes to this will I have without spending more money to go back to that team of lawyers and accountants who put my will together. Indeed this may have been the thinking of
Aubrey, the patriarch of a wealthy family who had dutifully spent a bundle
getting a solid will in place.

Aubrey's estate plan left everything to his spouse and maybe during
the meetings with his advisors, Aubrey missed one of the key reasons for
this plan, which was to take advantage of a very important Canadian tax-
planning option, the so-called spousal rollover. This rollover does exactly
what its shorthand name suggests: it allows the gains on capital property
to transfer or roll over to the surviving spouse so that capital gains tax will
only need to be paid when the surviving spouse sells the property or the
surviving spouse dies. As you can imagine, the spousal rollover is a really
important tax deferral mechanism in Canada, especially when millions are
at stake as in Aubrey's case.

However, in the year before his death Aubrey started to play around
with his will, by making handwritten addenda to it, and scribbles here,
there and everywhere on his will, with the end result that he "successfully"
changed his will such that his vast estate would be divided *equally* among
his wife, their children, the children's spouses and their grandchildren. And
while this distribution may sound fair and harmless, the end result was
devastating to the family: the tax bill was enormous because of the largely
forfeited spousal rollover and due to the simple math involved, Aubrey's
adult son, who had the most children of his own, received the lion's share
of the estate.

Was Aubrey of sound mind, you ask? Absolutely, no questions were
raised there. Did he hope to save his widow the difficulty of dividing the
estate in her will? Was he possessed of a desire to show through his will the
great love he had for all of his family including his children's spouses? Did
Aubrey realize the tax consequences? *Who knows?*

All we know is that both the family and the estate went through a very
difficult time. There was bitterness on the part of the widow, who saw her

future lifestyle change overnight with a much greater reliance on her children's "good will" than she would ever have expected, rafts of handwriting analyses, legal opinions and court applications, and—did we mention this already?—a much reduced estate than would have been in place had the spousal rollover applied to all of Aubrey's estate and not just the share that went to his widow.

There are many ways to go informal these days if you must: wear jeans to a funeral or send your thank-you notes by email. But don't mess around with the formalities of changing a will because the law of will making hasn't caught up to all those modern shenanigans quite yet.

points to take away

▶ The case law is full of court cases that look at people's attempts to change their wills, and so the law is rich with rules about how a will can or cannot be revised.

▶ Unfortunately, the best case is that the revision will work, but will create turmoil. The final result will likely still require your estate to go to court to have a judge review your alterations or add-ons and weigh the evidence about what you might have meant to do.

▶ The worst case is that your attempted revision has unintended consequences, ranging from revoking the whole will to increasing the tax bill to creating significant unhappiness in your family.

FIRST COMES LOVE, THEN COMES MARRIAGE . . .

MISTAKE #19

Neglecting to update your will as you enter marriage or a committed relationship

ISN'T NEW LOVE GRAND? Whether getting married or simply living happily together, life is bright and sunny when love is in the air . . . oh, happy sigh . . .

Okay, okay, enough already with the romance! To steer clear of this particular mistake, at some point in the midst of all this bliss, you need to review your estate planning and probably replace some or all of the documents, pronto. The type of planning required depends on your personal situation and relationship. It may include a cohabitation agreement if you are living with someone in a committed relationship but are not getting married, a prenuptial agreement if you are getting married, and in either case, wills, powers of attorney and personal directives. Even if you don't have a cohabitation agreement or a prenuptial agreement, a couple about to get married or living together in a committed relationship still needs to do estate planning.

Wills signed before the big wedding day must specifically state that they are made "in contemplation of marriage to Joe Boggs." Without an express statement that the wills are made in contemplation of the marriage, wills are revoked by marriage, a useful point to keep in mind if you have children from a first marriage whom you have carefully provided for in your existing will. Put another way, if you remarry thinking that the will you prepared some years earlier is perfect and still represents your wishes, you may be surprised to hear that your will is revoked the day you got remarried and you will die intestate—without a will.

Consider Michael who lost his wife, Penny, in 1995. Penny and Michael had two daughters, who are now adults and equal beneficiaries in Michael's will, which was prepared a couple of years after Penny's death.

When Michael married Sophie in 2009, they were both financially independent and content to leave their estates to their children from their first marriages rather than each other, so new wills were not prepared before their wedding. Michael and Sophie were unaware that their marriage revoked their wills and when Michael died a year later, he died intestate leaving his estate distribution subject to a combination of the rules of intestacy, family law rights and dependants' relief legislation.

Most likely, sorting out Michael's estate will require one or more court applications and possibly mediation or all-out litigation if the blended family cannot sift through the competing legal claims amicably.

At the same time as a couple thinking about marriage does will planning, the two partners need to think about beneficiary designations on registered plans, tax-free savings accounts and insurance; how they are holding all of their assets (as joint tenants or in their own names); and personal directives and powers of attorney.

points to take away

▶ Even though the law in Canada is intended to ensure that dependent children and spouses/partners—as those terms and relationships are defined in each province and statute—are looked after, the overall responsibility to make sure our wills properly reflect our intentions and our obligations rests on our own shoulders.

▶ A will is revoked by marriage unless the will states in the document itself that it is being signed in contemplation of a specific marriage.

▶ On a first and also subsequent marriage, a couple needs to think about getting new wills in place that not only cover the financial dynamics of their marriage but also recognize their intentions for children from earlier relationships and new stepchildren.

THEN COMES BABY IN THE BABY CARRIAGE!

MISTAKE #20

Not updating wills to reflect the life stages of your children

EVERY BOOK ON ESTATE PLANNING reminds us that the impending arrival of a new baby is a VERY IMPORTANT LIFE EVENT requiring a first or updated will. While that advice is sure true, the mistake we will discuss in this chapter is letting that flush of "estate-planning enthusiasm" fade over the years.

It does seem that people are most eager about will planning when the first child is on the way (oh yes, and on the eve of the skydiving adventure bought at a silent auction!). Maybe it is the excitement of being first-time parents that explains this burst of enthusiasm, but every estate lawyer is familiar with the panicked calls received shortly before the due date: "We need a will!"

Just as we all have hundreds of photos of our first child and then merely dozens of those that follow, parents' enthusiasm for updating their wills to accommodate changes in the family seems to wane over the years.

We were reminded of this when reviewing the comments from one of the lawyers who shared her thoughts for the book. She noted that she'd recently worked on an estate where the last will had been prepared when the deceased woman was married with several children. She later divorced and then had children in two other relationships but never remarried. When she died, her one and only will from her marriage was still valid because she lived in a province where a will is not revoked by divorce. Since she had never remarried, her first will had also never been revoked by marriage (as mentioned in Mistake #19). Furthermore, the deceased's adult children were financially independent and, in the province in question, did not have a claim against their mother's estate.

Referring to the deceased's children from her later relationships, our colleague succinctly said, "they were just out of luck." If these younger children had been under the age of majority when their mother died, they could have made a claim for support from her estate, but as they had just become of legal age, even that route was closed to them except for a possible claim for post-secondary education.

To complicate matters even further, you need to consider carefully how you define "children" in your life. Perhaps when you think about your children, in your mind, you are including your children's spouses in that definition, possibly children of your spouse (stepchildren), perhaps godchildren. It can get very complicated and it is important to make your intentions crystal clear in your will.

An interesting court case from Alberta looked at the issue of what people mean when they say "my children." The deceased in his will had left a small cash gift to each of "my children" followed by a list of nine people: two of his children, six stepchildren (none of them legally adopted by him) and one spouse of a child.

The residue, or remaining net worth, of the estate was then left in a lifetime trust for the deceased's third child, a disabled adult who was dependent on the deceased. Upon the disabled child's death, the remaining amount in the trust was to be divided among "my children," full stop. The question for the court to decide was whether the deceased intended "my children" in that part of the will to mean his legal children (two people) or the nine people he had described as "my children" in the cash gift paragraph of his will.

The court decided that the deceased had defined the people he considered as his children through the wording he used in the cash gift: a mixture of children, stepchildren and a child's spouse. The court noted, "The fact that his definition does not accord with a strict legal definition is of no relevance. It is his intention which is relevant."

Although the case is a good illustration of the importance of clearly defining who you mean when you refer to "children," don't infer from it that you can just include or exclude freely as you see fit. As you work through your estate planning with an experienced estate lawyer, you will be guided on how to successfully achieve your intentions. The personal relationship you have with the children in your life, broadly defined, may only be one relevant factor. Other factors that your lawyer will want to discuss with you include the financial relationship you have with any of them (i.e., are any dependent?) and the legislation in your province that pertains to providing for children after death.

So, review your will as the "children" in your life are born, grow up and marry, and not only from the simple perspective of whether they should be a beneficiary or not. Perhaps one adult child has developed skills that would make her a wise choice for your executor. Or maybe another adult child would be better served if you left his share in a trust rather than leaving it all to him outright. Your children's growth and maturity into adulthood and the people that they include in their lives are just two important examples of factors you need to consider as part of your estate planning.

As important as it feels to get a will in place that makes reference to your newborn son or daughter, don't stop there; often the more interesting and important planning for your children comes later as they grow up and mature, displaying new skills and attributes and bringing new people into their lives.

points to take away

▶ As we add children to our family and as they grow up, the provisions in our will should be tailored to their individual characteristics and needs.

▶ Don't take for granted that your notion of "your children" is clear; spell out to your lawyer whom you want to benefit and work with him or her to find a way in which to carry out your intentions as fully as possible.

▶ It is easy to forget that children can and should play a role in our estate plans once they become mature adults. In due course you will want to consider them for the role of executor or a co-executor of your estate and as a substitute decision maker under your power of attorney and personal directive.

IT WAS FUN WHILE IT LASTED!

MISTAKE #21

Neglecting to appropriately reflect separation and divorce in your estate plan

WHEN A LONG-TERM RELATIONSHIP ENDS, the last thing you might feel like doing is addressing your estate planning. But whether you were married or living together for a short time or a number of years, and whether you are simply separated right now or actually divorced, it is a big mistake to let your estate planning go unattended for long.

Emotions can run high when relationships end and sometimes this means people block out even thinking about estate planning or they get caught up in wanting to cut out the former spouse or partner from the will. Well, one general principle to bear in mind is that you can't get out of your legal obligations through your will any more than you can avoid your obligations while alive. You need to get good advice on addressing your new life and how it affects your will; failing to do so will invariably end up being more expensive to your estate than if you'd sought expert assistance.

As you move through a separation from a spouse or a partner with whom you lived, the law seeks to balance the parties' financial situation, guided by the interplay of federal divorce law and the provincial family legislation, and the many factors involved in each and every situation. If you die in the middle of the process, your estate remains responsible for your obligations to former spouses or partners, and dependent children, even if a separation agreement has not yet been reached. If a separation agreement *has* been signed, it may bind your estate to pay support obligations and your lawyer may recommend referring to it in your will. Even if your separation agreement does *not* specifically bind your estate, after your death the law may require your estate to pay ongoing child support obligations.

So what does all of this complexity mean to you if you are contemplating separation or going through it? Get advice on the best way to update your will to reflect the stage of your separation/divorce and then get to it! If you have an old will that leaves all or part of your estate to your former partner, you need to revise it with your lawyer's guidance so that your new intentions are balanced with your legal obligations.

Put another way, it is not an option to simply remove your former spouse or partner from your will. What you do in your will must be in synch with the stage you are at in your separation and divorce proceedings and the related agreements and court orders.

In some provinces a divorce revokes aspects of an existing will that benefit the former spouse, but other provinces treat the pre-divorce will as entirely valid. Neither result ensures a good outcome and either way, a will that predates a divorce is unlikely to be an accurate reflection of either the deceased's wishes or his or her obligations.

It's pretty obvious that the more complicated the situation (several relationships over the person's lifetime, children from a couple of those relationships), the more complicated the planning, but *failing* to plan creates a nightmare at the time of death.

While any post-separation estate planning to-do list will be incomplete because each situation is unique, points to cover with your estate-planning lawyer include:

- insurance coverage to address the terms of the separation agreement, such as the payment of spousal support for the rest of the former spouse's life, or specific maintenance payments for minor children;

- any and all court orders and agreements in place—some will need to be included expressly in your will, others will not;

- beneficiary designations on registered plans;

- assets that may still be held jointly with the former partner, or buy-sell agreements still in effect between you and a former spouse;

- personal directives; and

- powers of attorney, these last two documents being items that you could address and update as soon as you are separated. (Note that the terminology for personal directives and powers of attorney varies from province to province.)

points to take away

▶ If we separate from our partner or spouse, to minimize the confusion and potential for litigation arising at our death, it is essential that updated estate planning contemplate the legal obligations we have for all of our children and possibly our former spouse(s) or partner(s).

▶ The period during and just after separation and divorce is often a very "fluid" time when the parties' rights and obligations are being sorted out. Seek advice as to how to best reflect your new relationship with your "ex" while still meeting your obligations.

▶ Trying to do something in your estate planning that is more harsh than what is being negotiated or has been negotiated will only backfire, very possibly resulting in litigation over your estate.

YOU NEED A PLAN, STAN

MISTAKE #22

Neglecting to do appropriate planning for the death of key people in a privately held business or farm

IT'S A BIG MISTAKE when Mary and Beth, sisters and proud owners of Marybeth Widgets, put their heads in the sand about what happens when one of them dies. Privately held businesses are a "hot button issue" in estate planning, and from our discussions with a number of professionals, we gleaned that the controversy they can cause sometimes has less to do with the dollars at stake and more to do with interpersonal (often the all-in-the-family sort) dynamics and a healthy dose of emotion.

When we talk about privately held businesses, we are including partnerships, corporations and family farms, which can all generate conflict if enough attention isn't paid to planning for the death of the main people in charge.

There are four main mistakes made regarding privately held businesses and what happens when the key person dies:

- Communication: people don't talk about succession issues, much less the death issue. Ironically the worst offenders for not talking about these delicate topics are close friends and family members who are in business together.

- Documentation: if they do talk, they don't get their discussions and agreements reviewed or properly documented by professionals.

- Funding: shareholder agreements, if they are in place, can be useless if the cash to actually carry out the terms of the agreement is not available. For example, if the agreement directs the corporation or a surviving shareholder to buy the deceased shareholder's interest, the corporation or the shareholder, as applicable, must have the funds on hand or available through insurance in order to actually implement the deal.

- Updating: once completed, the agreements often become stale-dated and when the need for them arises, they do not achieve their intended purpose.

communication

One senior lawyer whom we contacted about this topic has an impressive track record of working with wealthy families as they sort their way through succession and estate planning. We expected to hear back from him about all sorts of technical details and the latest planning tips and strategies. Instead, his email note a week later said that since receiving our questions he hadn't been able to get off his mind a recent situation involving bitter estate litigation that had been commenced by those of the deceased's children who had not received an interest in the family business from their parents' estate.

The lawyer noted that these children had actually received more from the estate than their siblings but "they were excluded from the family business they had grown up in. I believe that if the parent had informed all the children of his choice during his life and explained his reasons, it might have ended differently, or at least led to a more equitable distribution of the estate."

But, you may be thinking, how can you have these conversations? Like the patriarch in our colleague's case, you may want to duck the difficult topics to do with your business, farm or partnership as long as possible—it may feel easier just to keep the peace. There could be a better way; although we tend to think about mediation as a process that people enter after a dispute starts, it can also be effectively used to hammer out a solution before illness or death makes the topic front and centre at the worst possible time.

Mediation involves all the parties creating a long list of options and solutions and then working together to combine them into a viable solution. Often parties have interests and concerns that others in the process may not have even been aware of, such as children who you assume want the business may in fact not be at all interested and the children who do want to be involved may be the ones that come up with the best ideas for how to compensate their siblings who will not receive a share of the business.

The point is not that mediation is *required* for you and your family or business partners to have difficult conversations, only that it is an option. And it is an option you should consider carefully if you and your family or business partners are caught in a difficult limbo between knowing something needs to be done and drawing up the agreement. There is not much point in retaining a professional to draft a terrific shareholders' agreement that you know will only cause grief. You somehow, some way, need to find a way to discuss the matter openly and productively before it can be committed to paper.

documentation

Once you and your family or other business partners have agreed to a plan in principle, the next step is to document the plan in whatever fashion is appropriate for your situation. This documentation will definitely include a will, and if there is more than one shareholder or partner in the business, a buy-sell agreement is required to direct what happens if a shareholder dies or is otherwise forced to leave the business, or chooses to leave the business.

The buy-sell agreement will cover questions such as:

- the events that will cause a buyout (such as death, disability, retirement, an owner leaving the business);

- the people who will be eligible to buy the departing or deceased shareholder's interest; and

- the price that will be paid for the interest in the company or the method by which the price will be calculated.

funding

When entrepreneurs have extra cash they tend to do the entrepreneurial thing, such as buy more land, build more buildings, renovate and upgrade. While this is clearly the way that businesses grow, this approach also means that when the buy-sell agreement is triggered by the death, disability or departure of a key person, neither the business nor the surviving owners have the cash to carry out the terms of the agreement. In other words, the buy-sell agreement is unfunded and is basically just a piece of paper.

This is where insurance comes in and it is something that you will want to think about and obtain early. A practical point to consider that was brought to our attention by an insurance executive is the issue of healthy shareholders with a normal weight who have to contend with a shareholder who is an obese smoker. *Awkward!* What would be impolite social conversation becomes an important and necessary business discussion in light of the importance of the key-person insurance and the disparity in premium costs between normal and high-risk insurance.

updating

It's essential to keep the documentation for the succession of your business or farm lined up with the insurance policy. Consider this situation: Two shareholders entered into a buy-sell agreement with $500,000 in life insurance on each life, payable to the operating company. The agreement provided that the spouse of the first deceased shareholder would sell her shares to the company and the company would buy back these shares at the value they were worth immediately before the death.

Over time, the business began to wind down, with the owners taking the value out of the operating company where the insurance was held. As fifteen years went by, the specific terms of the buy-sell agreement slipped everyone's mind, although if asked the shareholders would likely have agreed that the spouse of the first to die was to be paid at least half of the insurance.

However, at the first death, the value of the company—now a shell— was nominal and so, according to the agreement's terms, only a nominal amount was paid to the spouse of the deceased shareholder for her late husband's shares. Accordingly, almost all of the insurance proceeds ultimately went to the surviving and now sole shareholder. While all of this was within the written terms of the agreement, those terms had become seriously outdated over time as the business evolved from being an active company to merely a holding company.

points to take away

▶ The first and maybe most important step is to communicate with everyone involved. Avoid assumptions about who wants what. Get professional assistance in order to facilitate the discussions if you need to. Procrastinating in addressing the issues of passing on a privately held business, including the capabilities of your children, will not work over the long term.

▶ The value of a farm or business is often not available in cash, so consider how the buy-sell agreement will be funded or the terms of the will carried out to achieve the desired fair result. Investigate and secure any required life insurance early in the game.

▶ Keep your will, the buy-sell agreement and any related insurance up to date; even a few years is a long time in the life of a privately held business, and things change, especially the value of a business.

WELL, HE SURE CAN MIX A MEAN MARTINI!

MISTAKE #23

Selecting the wrong executor

THIS MISTAKE IS SUMMED UP well by a quote shared with us by a seasoned trust company professional: "A good executor can salvage a poor will and a poor executor can ruin a good one," meaning of course that having a well-drafted will only gets your estate so far. How the will is interpreted and used in the administration of your estate depends a great deal on the skill and wisdom of the executor you have named in it.

When we mention to people that we have written a book about the mistakes people make in estate planning, reactions fall into roughly two camps. The first is kind of a deer-in-the-headlights look that we've come to suspect means they are thinking something like, *Sheesh*, I don't have a will so that is Mistake #1 but what are the other 49 Mistakes?!

The other reaction is more reflective, the calm and detached question of people who have their estate planning wrapped up with a bow: "Hmm, that's interesting . . . so tell me, what is the *number one* mistake that people make?"

Well, like a parent who would never choose one child over the other, it is hard to decide on the number one mistake, but from our experience and that of the professionals we spoke to, this mistake is definitely in the running for top spot.

People think of the selection of their executor as just another item on the wills checklist. Right after the blank spaces for name, date of birth, address and specifics about the assets, a checklist often asks for the name of the executor (or co-executors) whom we want to appoint. And since many of us would rather be watching the Santa Claus parade on a freezing day in November than thinking about the day we die, we write down the name of someone or a couple of people in our inner circle to do the job, resolving to ask them if this will be okay, and move on to the next question. Later, if we think of it at all, we may decide: (1) the honour of being our executor is so great that we don't need to ask for his, her or their permission; (2) that a surprise element will work well in this situation; or (3) since we are named in their will, the question of asking for permission is moot.

The problem with this approach is simply that *the executor of our estate can muck up everything in myriad ways.* If we are taking the time to do a will, we should think long and hard about who is going to be the leader of the band.

One way to think about the job of an executor is to remember back to the last time you left someone to step into your shoes, figuratively speaking. If you're a parent, that may have been when you and your spouse took your first getaway and left the kids with their grandparents. Or if you own a small business or have a busy professional practice, it could have been as you left for some much needed R & R. Either way, you will remember the lists, the notes, the diagrams, the careful preparation to make sure that the baby's formula was organized for a whole week or that the discussions with the difficult client would go fine. We have no doubt you carefully spelled out all the people to contact and things to do if the entire free world collapsed while you were on the beach in Cancún.

Remember that? Well, if you worried that much on behalf of your designated "caregiver" when you were away for a week, you can see why we are suggesting caring a whole lot more when thinking about who is going to look after your estate when you die. Because let's face it, even though there are some people who do leave very detailed lists for their executor, most of us would find doing that a little gloomy. What you need to do instead is select an executor who can really step up and take over when you die, figuring out anything that you may have forgotten to post on the fridge.

We could wax on for pages about the executor's duties: planning the funeral, notifying people, doing paperwork, providing death certificates here, there and everywhere, tracking down and safeguarding assets, tracking down and talking to beneficiaries, transferring assets into the estate's name, talking to various government agencies, banks, insurance companies, doing more paperwork. As one widower said to us, "The things to do are endless," and in that particular situation, all of the deceased's assets were going to the surviving husband!

But simply perusing checklists of "Things Executors Need to Do" can actually lead you astray when you're thinking about your executor appointment. Any intelligent person can get a list, do the things on the list and eventually be done with it, especially if he or she hires some good help like an estate lawyer and a tax accountant. The missing element when people focus on the "doing" is the emotional side of an estate. Even if you insist your family never talks about feelings, almost every estate involves emotions, hidden or out in the open, and a truly effective executor will know this and handle that aspect of the estate administration well.

During the many conversations we had with estate lawyers and trust companies about executor selection, not one person said to us, "Gosh, you know, some executors forget to cancel the deceased's social insurance card. And advertising for creditors—some people just never get that done!" Instead, the comments they shared with us were about how executor appointments can be a disaster if the person named is not a good "fit" with the job—and it *is* a job, not an honour, not a figurehead role, a *job.*

Examples given to us of executor-appointments-gone-wrong include situations where the executor:

- didn't have the interpersonal skills to work with the beneficiaries effectively;

- was the oldest child in the deceased's family or perhaps a favourite child but lacked the personality to do the job or frankly the ability to effectively work with his or her siblings at such a difficult time; or

- may have had the skills to do the job but was overwhelmed by the emotional difficulty of dealing with the affairs of a person whose death they were deeply grieving.

We are not suggesting that you ignore for a moment the highly administrative function of being an executor, when you select yours. Being an executor is one time when we could all use a terrific assistant. But as onerous as the running around aspect is, likely the greater task of an executor is to have the emotional intelligence, the aplomb and the strength of character to sufficiently detach from the sadness and the emotions running high to do a great job of administering your estate.

If you are naming your executor or executors from your family or circle of friends, you need to weigh how they interact within your circle against the challenges that will arise for them—are they up for it? If we give to our executor selection at least the care we give to choosing someone to look after our little children or very important business when we go on a vacation, we'll be on the way to making a wise and thoughtful choice.

points to take away

▶ The selection of an executor is one of the most important decisions we make as we plan our estate.

▶ The role of an executor includes many responsibilities, tasks and things to do. It is important to choose someone who will be smart enough to complete all the tasks, get help as needed and ensure the work is carried out in a timely manner.

▶ Perhaps even more important, we would be smart to select a person who can work without a lot of direction and who possesses a good sense of what you would want and how you would want your estate, your will and your beneficiaries handled.

▶ The best executors have a good way with people, especially the people in your inner circle; the worst executors will not have the personality or fortitude to deal effectively with the issues and emotions that will inevitably arise.

I DON'T CARE IF JOHNNY IS IN JAIL, HE'S MY LITTLE BOY!

MISTAKE #24

Naming all your children as your executors

IT'S A REAL MISTAKE to let your unconditional and equal love for all of your children lead you down the path of naming all of them as executors of your estate. *Oh, we know* that Johnny and Rosanna are every bit as smart as your other three children. Really, the justice system was so unfair to Johnny on the one and only occasion he used marijuana, and very soon Rosanna's writing will take off and she'll be able to pay her own rent and buy her own groceries. Why, those two have hearts of gold!

Parental delusions are a wonderful thing, but it is a bonehead idea to name Johnny and Rosanna as two of your four executors, along with Bradley, the chartered accountant son, and Linda, the busy mom who is also running a successful small business.

The life challenges Johnny and Rosanna face aren't the only reason to think twice about naming all four children as your executors; some of the other reasons are:

- A team approach to administering an estate is often a poor idea, no matter who is on the lineup.

- The children will be faced with the difficult discussion about some of them renouncing the job—and failing that difficult decision, they'll face the cumbersome job of working together to get the job done as one big, happy family.

- The law requires that executors must act unanimously (unless the will states otherwise), so the big, happy family approach can and will be sorely tested.

Let's look at those issues more closely.

just too many . . .

The first problem is that an executor team is a bad idea in 99 percent of estates: by and large, a competent person is best left to his or her own devices to administer an estate. He or she can hire professional assistance as and when needed.

For example, an executor will likely want to use a lawyer to assist with getting the certificate from the court formally appointing him or her as the estate's administrator, and, depending on the estate assets, other advisors may be needed such as an accountant, investment advisor, real estate agent or antique valuator.

The reality is that administering an estate includes a lot of painstaking, detailed work. An executor needs good walking shoes to get around to all the banks and other places that need death certificates. The idea of going to a lawyer's office to hear the reading of the will and retiring as a family to an oak-panelled library to discuss the estate is a myth—a nice one taking us back to a Dickensian era, but a myth nonetheless.

renunciation

A person named as an executor in a will is not required by law to accept the job. In other words, the executor can decide to renounce the appointment, so long as he or she has not intermeddled in the estate, *intermeddling* being a wonderful legal term that roughly means, "sticking your nose into the estate and doing stuff." Armed with this knowledge, you might assume that you can merrily appoint all of your children in your desire to be fair and loving, knowing that maybe the situation after your death will look after itself because a few of them will renounce.

Hang on there . . . in our experience, families that are smart enough to decide to do this are ironically the ones that likely could forge on and do a good job working together. They get together after the dust has settled after the funeral and agree that while it was very nice of Mom and Dad to name the whole lot of them, they wisely realize that it makes the most sense to let Bradley do the heavy lifting while the rest of them watch from the sidelines. They understand that there is a difference between being one of the executors and being a beneficiary. After the dust settles, they will all share equally in the estate.

On the other hand, those siblings who will need combat gear after a month or two of working together are the ones who insist they all need to be involved.

So don't shift the responsibility for being responsible to your kids—chances are good that your approach will backfire.

unanimity

There are all sorts of ways you can state in your will that your executors do not need to all agree, the simplest being a statement that the majority of executors agreeing on a course of action will carry the day. But parents who dither about naming only one or two children rather than all of them are also inclined to think that their kids will come to a magical consensus on everything from dividing up the heirloom china to selling the cottage at Red Deer Lake. Getting that consensus is probably unlikely and even if you do include a majority-vote clause in your will, think about the children who are not in the majority: hurt feelings will occur every time this happens.

points to take away

▶ It is perfectly normal to love your children equally and to want this to be demonstrated in your will, but think through the real-life, real-time consequences of naming all your children as your executors.

▶ Naming all of your children as your executors can be a landmine even if your estate should be relatively simple. Never underestimate the damage that can be done when people fight and emotions are involved.

▶ If it is at all feasible to do so during your estate-planning process, have an open discussion with your family as to whom you are naming as your executor or executors, why, and how all of your children will be treated equally (if that is the case!) in the *distribution* of your estate.

MOMMA ALWAYS SAID, "LIFE IS LIKE A BOX OF CHOCOLATES, YOU NEVER KNOW WHAT YOU'RE GONNA GET"

MISTAKE #25

Failing to consider a corporate executor and trustee when appropriate

SO HERE'S THE PROBLEM. It's not that our kids, siblings or close friends can't do most or all of the jobs of being an executor. File taxes? Check. Close bank accounts. Sure. Clean out and sell the house. Of course. Likely you have seen the people you want as your executor do all those very things and do them well. It's just that the job of an executor is often greater than the sum of its parts. Why? Some reasons that may or may not apply to you are:

- because your kids have fought all their lives and won't stop once you're gone, in fact the acrimony will likely get worse after your death;

- because your children get along fine but their spouses seem to cause dissension for some reason you have never quite understood; and

- because even though the executor's job is often described as work for a smart, energetic, do-it type, even a person with those attributes sometimes falls apart when Mom or Dad or a beloved sibling dies.

The executor's job can be likened to that of a parent. If a busy mom or dad wrote out the list of responsibilities she or he shoulders, the list would be daunting, but doable. But as a parent knows, the challenge of the job is understood only in the doing. No cheerful parenting book can describe the utter exhaustion of the first few months, the stress when both kids are wrestling in the living room mere seconds away from injury, or the gnawing worry of waiting for a teen with a new driver's licence who is late from a night out. In short, a list of parenting "jobs" can never really describe parenting and neither can the most comprehensive executor's task list describe being an executor. It is more than a list of things to do, and often we have blinders on to that truth when we select loved ones to be our executor.

In Jean's experience in leading a trust company, there are usually three main reasons given as to why people might want to consider a corporate executor (in Canada, this means a chartered trust company) to administer their estates. The first is that their children or other loved ones might be too busy, the second that the estate is very large or complicated, and the third that there is a potential for conflict during the estate administration.

When we look carefully at those three reasons for thinking about a corporate executor (i.e., others are too busy/it is complicated/there's conflict), if the first two scenarios exist and you nevertheless appoint a loved one to be your executor, your estate can often still have a satisfactory ending. In such situations, the too-busy or overwhelmed executor often has the good sense to either hire an agent, like a trust company, to assist them or if there is another executor named in the will who has the time and ability, then the too-busy person may simply renounce the job (i.e., not accept the appointment at the death) and let the other named executor carry on.

However, when *conflict* is the problem, rational thought seems scarce. Whether executors are fighting between themselves or with any of the beneficiaries (whom they likely are related to or know well), conflict seems to prevent the executors from either voluntarily removing themselves from the situation or doing an effective job administering the estate.

One trust officer we spoke with was working on an estate where the deceased had named his two sons to be the executors. There was absolutely no trust between the sons, and two years after their father's death, nothing had really been accomplished other than going to court to resolve one of their several disputes over the interpretation of the will.

Usually an estate just hires one lawyer if something in the will needs interpreting but since the two brothers/executors didn't agree on anything, each of the brothers hired a separate lawyer (at the estate's expense). With calmer heads now prevailing, it was agreed that a trust company should be appointed to manage the estate while the litigation worked its way through the system. As the trust officer dryly noted, "They still hate each other but at least they have us to run interference and try to get something done on their dad's estate."

You might be thinking that maybe Dad didn't realize his sons didn't get along, but lawyers and will planners with the trust companies tell a different story. They will tell you that clients often acknowledge their children's disagreements and differences but then quickly add that "when I'm gone, they will work it out." That's right, and there's never going to be any more shouting in the House of Commons either.

What usually happens when those same clients pass away is that the gloves really come off. Mix together years of disagreements, in-laws with their own opinions, disappointment over some parts of the will, and Grandma's missing tea set . . . well, you get the picture. One experienced estate administrator put it like this, "People think that their death will be the ultimate bonding time for their kids but it just doesn't work that way."

Only you know the people in your life and only you can decide if they are up for the job. Everything we've said above may simply not apply to you and your family. But if you have any doubt at all, the time spent speaking with a representative of a corporate executor may be worth it. He or she can take you through what will likely be required in your estate and discuss the value that a corporate executor could add, either named as the sole executor of your estate or as a co-executor with one of your loved ones. You may decide that it is not for you, but come away from the meeting with a better appreciation for the work that your executor or executors will take on. On the other hand, you may conclude that a corporate executor is one of the best-kept secrets of estate planning.

points to take away

▶ A corporate executor is commonly recommended when an estate is expected to be complicated; when potential individual executors live far away or are busy; or where there is a possibility of conflict. Each of these situations indicates that the appointment of a corporate executor (as sole executor or as a co-executor) may be wise.

▶ During will planning, parents often try to convince themselves that family conflict will be resolved after they die and that their children will get along well enough to administer the estate.

▶ In fact, long-standing sibling rivalry rarely stops when the parents are gone and is a frequent cause of estates in crisis.

▶ Executors who fight among themselves or with the beneficiaries, or who are unable to manage conflict among the beneficiaries, can prolong the estate administration for a very long time and wind up costing the estate much more in legal and other professional fees than should have been spent.

▶ Consider talking to a trust company about its services if you have any questions about the time, ability or interpersonal skills of any of the possible choices for your executor, even if those people are the very people that you love the most.

"... BOND. JAMES BOND."

 MISTAKE #26

Not being open about your executor appointment or not letting your executor know where to find the will or the required information

WE'VE REALLY INCLUDED TWO MISTAKES in this chapter, which can happen in a book that sets out to talk about the biggest estate-planning mistakes; somehow "51 mistakes" doesn't sound quite as catchy as "50." In any event, the first mistake is simply not telling your executor at all that he or she is named as an executor in your will, and the second and certainly related mistake is not leaving a road map for the executor to follow when you die. If you make both mistakes, it is double the trouble.

The first mistake—failing or forgetting to mention the appointment at all—is often made because people believe the named person will be so honoured by the appointment that there is just no doubt that he or she will accept it. A lot of people have a trilogy of requests in life: "stand up for me at my wedding; be the godparent (or some other mentoring type of person) to my child; be my executor." Who says no to those things? Maybe we are biased but it seems to us that wearing a too-tight tuxedo or ghastly lime green dress for a day pales in comparison to the responsibility of being the executor of an estate.

The second mistake—not leaving sufficient information behind for your named executor—refers to the information you leave for your executor for his or her review and assistance when you die. As we discussed in Mistake #17, sharing a copy of your will (and thus all of its contents) may or may not be wise for everyone at every stage of life, but it is *always* smart to leave a path that your executor can easily follow when you actually die.

If you are fortunate enough to be enjoying fantastic health right now, you may think that it is wise insurance to have a will but that it would be overdoing the whole planning thing to also gather up information as if you might die next week: *Good heavens, I certainly won't be dying next week!* Well, we hate to break it to you, but that is likely what most people think the week before they die, so if you are going to the trouble of preparing a will, go the extra mile and assemble an information package for your named executor.

Failing to leave the right information for your executor is quite easy to avoid if you understand why disclosure is important. Think about these points:

- Unless your executor is a trust company, there is going to be some level of shock, grieving and uncertainty for your executor upon news of your death. More information rather than less is always going to be best for a loved one in that state.

- Your affairs may be straightforward to *you* but in big part that is because it's *your* life! Think about your executor waking up one morning to learn of your death and trying to find, for example, the phone number of the best person to talk to in your employer's human resources department. Trying to get through to the switchboard could take two hours alone.

- Asking someone to be your executor is not just about you. Almost every executor wants to do the best possible job, but getting direction as to what the job is, and how exactly you would like to see it done, greatly increases the odds of the person feeling good about the work he or she does for you.

Let's look at the various types of disclosure you can consider, from bronze to gold medal level.

bronze medal disclosure

The basic, minimum information your executor should readily find at your death is the location of both the original will and a copy. In Mistake #17, we recommended storing your original will with the lawyer who assisted you with it, the trust company named in it to be an executor, or in a safety deposit box. As well, it is very important to then put a *copy* of the will where it can be easily found by your executor, such as in a filing cabinet or in a drawer in your home. On that copy, write the location of the original will, as well as the names and direct phone numbers of the relevant people who can assist your executor to retrieve the original, such as your lawyer, trust company professional or bank manager.

silver medal disclosure

One step up from the basic information about your will's location is leaving what trust company professionals call "the red binder" about your life. The professionals who shared that term with us also went on to emphasize that a "red binder estate" runs much more effectively and efficiently than any other type of estate. So what is this red binder? It is one location for every-thing that your executor will need to carry out the administration of your estate. And of course it needn't be red or even a binder—just remember that it is a collection of easily accessed information about your affairs. If this information is something you prefer to assemble electronically, you need to ensure that your executor has all of the necessary passwords to access your computer.

You will want to assemble:

- copies of your most recent power of attorney, personal directive and will

- names and addresses of all of your beneficiaries

- details about all of your assets: what they are, where they are, who has access to them, access information such as passwords and account num-bers, recent statements

- details about your debts and liabilities

- details about your insurance policies

- contact information about everyone and every company that should be notified on your death, such as vendors, suppliers, and credit card companies
- contact information for anyone else who may be involved in or helpful to the administration of your estate.

The simple act of annually updating this binder may ensure that your will planning really works. For example, forgetting about an insurance policy payable to the estate can throw a wrench into careful planning that did not contemplate a million dollars flowing into the estate!

While all of this record keeping may sound onerous, once set up, it will be a simple process to update it annually.

gold medal disclosure

If you want to give your executor every opportunity to succeed, in addition to the steps mentioned above, you will leave written letters or memoranda, which are not legally binding but which share your views on:

- Your funeral and burial. This is best communicated while you are alive, but sometimes a deceased person's family resists certain funeral and burial directions, such as cremation, even if they were informed of these wishes ahead of time. Make it a little easier on everyone by setting out your views in writing in the will and, if more details are desired or required, in a written document for your executor.
- The distribution of personal effects that you would like to see. Although they are not binding directions since they are not a part of your formal will, your executor and your beneficiaries will be very grateful for any statement of your wishes on who gets what.
- If you have not discussed all of your will planning with your beneficiaries, your thoughts on why your will says what it does. Heartache or perhaps even litigation can be averted by your written explanation as to why you have left one child's inheritance in trust and the other child's as an outright gift, for example. Or why a large portion of your estate is going to charity. Our advice is to communicate any of these decisions while you

are alive, but if that doesn't work for you, consider written statements to be shared by your executor with your beneficiaries after you are dead.

- How your children should be raised and how your wishes about that tie into the trust provisions set out in your will. For example, in your will itself you may provide that money be paid to the guardian so that the children can attend private school. In the letter—which is a statement of your wishes and not a binding document—you can assist both the trustee and the guardian by sharing your views on which children most need private education and which schools you believe would benefit them the most.

- Any other thoughts, views, wishes or statements that may ease your executor's workload or decision making, or assist your family, friends or other beneficiaries in understanding your will and the estate administration.

points to take away

▶ There is more to picking an executor than simply asking him or her to say yes. It is essential that both you and the chosen executor understand the importance of the role.

▶ No matter how healthy we are, the reason for estate planning is to cover off the unlikely chance of an unexpected or early death. Therefore it makes sense to go one step further and assemble the information that our executor needs to do good work.

▶ You will at least want the executor to know where both the original will and a copy are located and how to gain access to them easily.

▶ A better approach is to leave detailed information about our life so the executor can act most effectively and efficiently.

▶ Although a well-drafted will ensures that the desired structure of our estate is clear, additional direction from us will enhance the understanding of the will not only by our executor but also our beneficiaries even though such memoranda aren't legally binding on our estate.

KUM BAY YA, MY LORD, KUM BAY YA

MISTAKE #27

Failing to think through how the executors will make decisions

IT'S EASY TO SEE HOW people make the mistake of not thinking carefully about how the executors will work together. The tendency to think superficially about our will is hard to fight: we select our executors and then block out thoughts about the actual work they will be doing. What they'll be doing of course is liquidating our assets, paying our debts and eventually distributing what is left to our beneficiaries in accordance with our will. This work will inevitably lead to situations where all of the executors may not agree.

But making this mistake of not thinking about how your executors will work together is like deciding to build a house, selecting a builder and a plan and then concluding you are done. Anyone who has built a new home will know differently: there are about 640 decisions left to make, from selecting hardware for the kitchen cabinets to choosing tiles for the lower level laundry room, and all those decisions add up, transforming blueprints into your own beautiful home.

To avoid the mistake we're looking at in this chapter, the first thing you need to ask yourself is whether it is necessary to have more than one executor in the first place: if you only have one executor, he or she will agree with himself or herself 100 percent of the time.

appointing a sole executor

If you are thinking that the complexity of your affairs requires two or more people to figure out your estate, well, we should point out that we assume Canada is a pretty complicated country to run, yet there is only one prime minister—and there's only one president of the United States, and only one chief executive officer running each of Canada's largest corporations. Do these people do it all themselves, staying up all hours of the night? No, we hope not; instead they have hordes of staff and a plan for how the work will be done with the ultimate responsibility rolling up to the boss.

These are extreme examples but they make the point. Too often people name multiple executors not because they really think the estate will be terribly difficult, but because they don't want to hurt anyone's feelings, or they're unsure what is going to be involved, so rather than take a chance, they just throw in several names as co-executors. Unfortunately, if the executors hit a bump in the path and cannot agree on decisions, having only one executor would have been the better choice.

One suggestion that works nicely in some situations is where the executor appointment clause includes a paragraph requesting the executor to consult with certain people about certain issues. For example, perhaps there is a person who could really assist with the distribution of the personal effects or a long-standing accountant who is to be consulted on the deceased's tax and business affairs.

If you decide to use this approach, though, the key point for you and your drafting lawyer is to make sure that the directions don't morph into appointing more executors. One situation we heard about involved the children of the deceased as the executors (i.e., the decision makers) but every decision they made on payments out of some of the trusts had to be agreed to by three church pastors who had been close to the deceased. So who was the boss? In an estate it should be the executors, but in such a situation where the executors' decisions can be overruled, it becomes very unclear and *a lack of clarity in an estate is a bad thing.*

appointing two or more executors

If, in the final analysis, you decide to name two or more executors, then this is when you need to address how they will make decisions. The law on executor decision making is that the executors must act unanimously unless the will stipulates otherwise. Reasonable people who are committed to working together in the best interest of the estate will not have a problem with this; consensus can always be reached if people want to reach it and are aware that the alternative route is to seek the advice and direction of the court, requiring a daunting amount of time and money.

If the idea of always having to reach agreement strikes you as unnecessary Kum Bay Ya, then one option is to ask your lawyer to draft a majority clause whereby decisions can be made with only a majority of the executors in agreement. For example, if you have named your spouse, your eldest child and your former business partner as your three executors, you will want to think about whether one of the executors, like your spouse, should always be in the majority.

Often when a trust company is appointed as one of several executors and there is a majority clause, the corporate executor will insist on the clause stipulating that the trust company's vote must be in the majority; otherwise it could end up being liable for (and having the deep pockets to cover) decisions with which it did not agree in the first place.

points to take away

▶ Appointing only one executor will eliminate the hazards of multiple executors who argue over everything. Ask yourself if you really need to appoint more than one executor.

▶ One option to think about is providing for advisors to your executor on issues about which a corporate executor or a sole executor may not have sufficient knowledge. However, be sure that it is clear in your will that the role of the advisors is to provide guidance and suggestions only so that there is no confusion that the ultimate decision making lies with the executor.

▶ If you do decide on more than two executors, consider including a majority-rule clause so that a stand-off is avoided.

AND NO RED BULL AFTER 6 P.M.!

MISTAKE #28

Failing to adequately prepare for the possibility of dying when your children are young

PEOPLE MAKE A MIXED BAG of mistakes when it comes to minor children and estate planning. These errors include:

- failing to mention all of their minor children;
- stalling on their will because they can't agree on a guardian;
- choosing an inappropriate guardian or trustee; and
- not giving sufficient directions for the period of time in which the children are being raised by the guardian.

failing to mention some of their minor children

We're not referring here to the storyline in the *Home Alone* movie where the parents somehow managed to not account for little Kevin as they sped off to the airport. We're talking about parents who haven't acknowledged one or more of their minor children in their will, usually because the children have not been acknowledged publicly at all. This situation happens more often than you think: "there's nothing new under the sun," and if you or someone you know is in this situation, there is very little upside to not sharing this information with the lawyer helping you with your will. Estate-planning lawyers have seen everything and an experienced lawyer will be able to walk you through your available options. The final decision of course will be yours.

Clear-eyed estate planning requires even delicate situations to be included in your discussions; not addressing them may feel easier now but could have the effect of suspending your estate in litigation on behalf of the unacknowledged minor child or children for a good length of time. Enough said on that one.

stalling on the will because of indecisiveness about a guardian

For absolute clarity here, the *guardian* of your children named in your will would, if you died, step into your shoes for the personal care, housing, feeding, educating, passing-on-values aspects of parenting; the *trustee* would manage the money you have left for the children, ensuring it is used wisely while they are young with as much as possible left when they reach the age specified in your will.

Without a shadow of a doubt, parents stall more on who should be named as the guardian of their minor children than any other aspect of their will planning, including the naming of the executor and trustee.

It is a little ironic that the guardianship decision so often takes such deliberation since it is not a binding decision in any event. As we mentioned in Mistake #12, the court has the final say on who will be the guardian of your children and it is possible that in the years between signing your will and your untimely death:

- your named guardian may have moved;

- your children may be old enough to express a different perspective to the court as to who should be their guardian; or

- the person you've named may simply not be appropriate any longer.

So, try not to let the decision between your sister, Ann, and your best friends, Sue and Chris, hold up the entire freight train of your will planning.

There really are very important reasons to get a will done over and above the guardianship appointment. It just isn't smart to hold off forever on finalizing those draft wills on your night table simply over who should be named as the children's guardian.

choosing an inappropriate guardian or trustee

Having droned on about *getting on with a decision* about your children's guardian, we'd be remiss to not point out that sometimes the guardianship and trusteeship appointments for bereaved children aren't as wise as they should have been.

The key point with the guardianship appointment is to keep it fresh; the ideal guardians when your children are 3 and 5 may not be the best ones when they are 13 and 15. Facing an application to formally appoint guardians of teens, the court will most likely ask the children for their opinion, so it is best to have a selection in your will that makes sense not only to you but to your children as they mature and develop. Eventually of course your children will reach the age of majority and an updated will won't even mention guardians. Until then, keep the clause current.

Regarding the appointment of a trustee for your children's inheritance, here the tip is to ensure that your named trustee is always a person of unquestioned integrity and financial acumen. If the trustee of your children's trusts has a gambling addiction or for some other reason squanders or inappropriately manages the money, it will be very difficult later for the children to get it back: there isn't a magical fund in the government or elsewhere that will compensate your children for their lost inheritance. If the trustee has spent not only your children's assets but also has burned through all of his or her net worth, there won't be a happy ending.

not providing direction on the guardianship period

Once the challenging decision is made about who should be the children's guardian, parents' wills often become vague on things like housing, transportation and the scope of payments to and on behalf of the children, such as private school tuition.

To avoid a direct conflict of interest, many professional advisors suggest that your children's guardian (the person who makes the personal care decisions and the decisions about how to raise the children) and your children's trustee (the money manager) be different people. Nevertheless, the guardian and trustee will need to work hand in hand to raise the children, and some flexible directions about the type of expenditures you see as appropriate may be very helpful.

In Jean's experience, some parents wish to be very clear on the importance of things such as:

- the guardians being able to renovate their home in order to have room to include the children of the deceased;

- buying a larger vehicle;

- continuing to send the children to private schools; and

- providing travel money so that the children can visit grandparents.

If you are thinking provisions like these make sense, raise them with your lawyer, but keep in mind that you don't want your will to be so very specific that it becomes inflexible. At most you want to provide guidelines, not an itinerary for every week. It's also important to keep in mind that the more specific you get, the more often you will need to revisit your will. While it may make sense to suggest the guardians do reasonable renovations to their home when your children are toddlers, by the time your kids are teenagers, you'd likely want to rethink having this type of expenditure suggested in your will. The best advice in any area of unique will drafting is this: retain good help. A lawyer who focuses his or her practice in estate planning will be well equipped to assist you with direction you wish to include in planning for your minor children.

points to take away

▶ Minor children have a significant claim on their parents' estate and so the best approach for parents is to spend time ensuring that their wills adequately address their minor children.

▶ Experienced estate planners have seen it all, from children who are not publicly acknowledged to others who have serious mental or physical challenges. The best approach is to be open and upfront about your minor children and their unique characteristics so as to get the best advice.

▶ Because of the importance of having a will in place if you have minor children when you die, don't stall forever on whom to appoint as your child's guardian. However, understand the characteristics that you need in a guardian and a trustee, and make wise choices that reflect your values and your children's characteristics.

HE LOOKS SO CUTE IN HIS SUIT AND TIE!

MISTAKE #29

Not thinking through the ramifications of giving property to minor children

A LOT OF PARENTS MISTAKENLY THINK that all sorts of neat and innovative estate planning can be done by having their young children hold assets or money in their own names. Whether it is a misguided attempt to save tax or a cute way to encourage early investment acumen, more often than you might think, parents put shares in their small business or bank accounts into their kids' names (or "in trust," whatever the heck that means) only to regret it later.

If, like us, you read tabloid magazines while standing in the grocery checkout line, you'll notice that child actors and teen pop idols fight a lot with their parents. It's just a wild guess but we're pretty sure that some of the drama revolves around money. Even young people who are rich and famous can't control money if they haven't reached the age of majority—and neither necessarily can their parents, although parents from the beginning of time have assumed that what belongs to their kids belongs to them.

And as we say, even the not-so-rich-and-famous crowd can get caught up in thinking that assets in their kids' own names sound like a great idea. Perhaps parents think that ultimately they themselves will be able to direct the transfer of the assets out of the names of the children but that's not how it works. If your minor children hold shares in your private company and you decide it is time to do a complicated reorganization, good luck with that. One estate lawyer we spoke with said she had seen situations like this involving thousands of dollars in professional fees. If the children are under the age of majority, the appointment of a guardian or trustee (the wording will depend on your province of residence) is required and then the appointed guardian or trustee needs to be at the table ensuring that the reorganization makes sense for the minor child.

The other situation that can strike fear in a parent's heart is when a child is nearing the age of majority and the parent realizes that he or she will soon be able to claim the bank account that has been building up at a nice clip over the years. Somehow when our kids are babies we just can't imagine the faraway day when they will be adults. Then that birthday when our child becomes legally an adult is right there in our face, as is the luxury car dealership.

Restrain yourself when it comes to putting assets into your children's own name, or get advice on how to do it and what the ramifications will be down the road. As the author Gretchen Rubin puts it about the brevity of our children's youth: "the days are long but the years are short."

points to take away

▶ Minor children cannot manage their own assets, no matter how mature they may seem, and neither can their parents direct, without court approval, the transfer of assets that have been placed in the names of the children.

▶ Get professional advice about putting assets, such as the shares of your family business, into your children's names; if you put assests in their names without clearly thinking it through, the future result may be an expenditure of significant time and money.

I LOVE YOU ALL THE WAY TO THE MOON AND BACK

MISTAKE #30

Making the assumption that after your death your beneficiaries will understand why you have done what you did

IT SURE IS A MISTAKE to think other people can read our minds. They can't—and their skill at it doesn't improve after we are dead. Estate and trust professionals often see estate situations where the deceased person's family, friends or colleagues simply can't understand why they were treated as they were (or weren't) in the will. In our conversations with these professionals, we heard time and again about attempts people had made to treat their beneficiaries fairly, instead creating irreparable animosity after the death when the wills' contents were revealed.

In some cases of course, people intend to create conflict. Leona Helmsley, dubbed the "Queen of Mean" by employees in her hotel empire, explicitly excluded two grandchildren in her will "for reasons which are known to them." *Okay then!* No doubt Helmsley, who appeared to thrive on conflict, would have possessed a sense of the outrage this exclusion would cause.

But using a will as a sword is more for the movies and romance fiction than for real life in Canada. Real life in Canada involves most people trying their best to be fair. Unfortunately, attempts to use wills as a way to "even things up" can backfire if the strategies don't line up with the beneficiaries' individual recollections of history.

Most of the situations we describe involve families and often families don't talk out loud about what's fair and what isn't. So it may be hard for you to even envision some of the challenging situations that can occur in the pursuit of parents trying to be fair to everyone. Some common examples to get you thinking are:

- An adult child's long-standing residency with Mom may be viewed by that child as giving up her life for Mom's well-being but seen as free-loading by her siblings after the child receives Mom's house in the will.

- Similar but slightly different is the situation where one child lives nearby the parents and is the primary caregiver and go-to person. Giving that child a larger share in the will may be an attempt by the parents to compensate him or her for carrying out this emotionally, physically and (sometimes) financially draining role, but the children who live far away may not see it that way at all.

- A child who never had children of his own may receive a larger share to compensate for the money spent by his late parents on his siblings' children (the deceased's grandchildren) over the years—but once again, this may not be seen as fair by the children who get the smaller share in the will. They may have forgotten all about the summer camps, trips to Europe and other expenses paid for their kids by Mom and Dad.

- The family business going to the one or two children who worked in it may feel like fair compensation to those children, but the rest of the children may wonder why their share of the estate is smaller unless the distribution of the remaining amount of the estate (after the family business is transferred) is shared disproportionately in their favour.

- A larger share to the child who is not as financially successful as his or her siblings may feel completely fair to a loving and worried parent but be viewed as nothing less than painfully hurtful to the children who receive less. They may view their financial success as something they have worked very hard to achieve and feel punished by receiving less than their sibling.

Here's the really sticky part about these examples: each of the viewpoints we've suggested makes some sense—each and every one! In an emergency, you may drive well over the speed limit, but, face it, an observer will just think you are a maniac behind the wheel. Similarly people may very well have a different perspective than you do on their place in your will.

Dr. Margaret MacAdam is president of the Age Advantage and has a Ph.D. in health policy and aging. She has devoted her career to the challenging macro-issues of an aging population. But as hard to solve as those big-picture issues are, when we spoke with Dr. MacAdam, she expressed her frustration at the micro-issue of family conflict after Mom and Dad have died. Like many professionals in law, accounting and trust services, Dr. MacAdam commented on the apparent inability of so many families to avoid strife over a parent's estate. She joined the chorus of estate professionals who mostly had one word for us on this issue: *communicate!*

It is unlikely that you want to get your loved ones all in a lather à la Queen of Mean. It is also really unlikely that beneficiaries who are all related to you in the same way, notably your children, will understand your reasoning if you decide to do some equal-is-not-fair type of planning. To carry out this type of planning, you need to:

- obtain advice as to whether your intentions are likely to be in line with provincial legislation about providing for children (a couple of provinces limit the ability of parents to treat their children unequally); and

- think about how to communicate what you are planning to do.

At the risk of sounding cheeky, you have two choices about when to communicate to the beneficiaries of your will: before you die or after.

communicating before your death

All things being equal, bringing the issue out in the open while you are alive and competent may be the best tactic. In fact, talking about your will early and often may eventually wear down your kids to see it your way and by the time you pass away, the whole estate plan will be old news.

And who knows? Maybe your children, individually or together, will have some great ideas as to how your objective of fairness can best be achieved. Just be sure to run any such suggestions past your advisor because some "great ideas" can have horrible tax or other unexpected consequences.

communicating after your death

Even though talking is terrific and allows for a back-and-forth discussion, we can imagine situations where people feel they simply can't raise certain issues with their kids. We won't delve deeply into why that may be—this is a book on estate planning after all, not a psychology textbook. But we accept that a Sunday afternoon family meeting about wills isn't for every family. Even so, you can still work with your lawyer to put together an ancillary document to be stored with your will, providing some details behind your thinking.

Why bother with all this communication? The main reason of course is to minimize unhappiness and hard feelings after you die by providing your personal perspective in a way that the wording in a will can't achieve. When people are upset with the contents of a will, they tend to take out their anger on others: the estate executor, the other beneficiaries, the deceased's lawyer, the cat-sitter, whoever happens to be around. A written statement of your love for your children and why you are providing for some children differently than others will direct the focus where it should be: on you, your thoughts, the wealth you have amassed during your lifetime and how you see that wealth being appropriately distributed at your death.

Communication about the reasons behind your planning will not necessarily make everyone happy. However, the probability of hurt feelings or even litigation can be reduced if Mom or Dad, for example, share their candid thoughts and plans about their wills while they are alive, rather than leave it all as a big surprise for after their death.

points to take away

▶ Over the years, certain dynamics can cause you to consider providing for one beneficiary in a different manner than others you care about.

► Although most Canadian provinces allow parents of adult, financially independent children to leave them whatever share of the estate the parent wishes to leave, if you are thinking of an unequal distribution, it's essential to consult with an estate lawyer to ensure that this can be achieved in accordance with the legislation in your province.

► Although your reasons for your estate planning may make good sense to you, if the planning comes as a surprise to the people that you care about, or once cared about, it can cause tremendous heartache and result in the possibility of avoidable estate litigation.

► Communicating your plans to your beneficiaries, especially your adult children or grandchildren, while you're alive or working with your lawyer on a document to be read after your death are two ways to think about approaching "unique" planning in your will.

► The final point to take away is this: *it is your will after all.* Even with the best of intentions and professional advice, you may not be able to avoid conflict or even a court challenge to your estate plan. In some situations, you may just need to accept that one or more of your beneficiaries won't be happy.

THAT'S NOT A MOSQUITO, THAT'S YOUR SISTER-IN-LAW!

MISTAKE #31

Not dealing appropriately with the family's recreational property

AH, THE FAMILY COTTAGE. The smell of the lake, the quiet sunrise in the morning, the fresh air, the laughter . . . ***THUD!!***

Sorry, but that's the sound of you coming down to earth when you really begin to think about passing the lovely recreational property on to the kids, or sharing the place with your siblings. Coming from Saskatchewan, Jean thinks of these properties as *cabins*, whereas Sarah is familiar with the term *country houses*. Call them what you like, but when we reviewed all the commentary we received on the family-cottage topic from trust and estate professionals, it began to look mighty appealing to suggest renting a place whenever your family feels like hanging out together.

We also found it interesting that although estate-planning articles and books tend to focus on the *tax* issues arising with a cottage, the stories we heard most often about cottage disputes after death didn't involve taxation at all.

Let's look at each of the issues one at a time.

the "parents' presence" issue

For most, the family cottage is much more than an asset; it represents a wealth of wonderful memories, with many circling around Mom and Dad's presence as parents and later as hosts and grandparents. Once they no longer visit as much or have passed away, the persona of the cottage can change, not always in a positive way. Something as innocuous as who sleeps in the master bedroom and who gets the basement can become emotional hot buttons.

It's tempting to ignore this point as something that is too vague or wishy-washy to mention. On the other hand, it's a point for consideration: the absence of the parents at the same time as a family is trying to sort out how they are going to share the cottage in the future is often a very challenging combination.

ownership traps

There are two ways to own real estate with other people: joint tenancy and tenancy in common. Joint tenancy means that when one joint tenant dies, the remaining joint tenants take the deceased person's share. Tenancy in common means that each tenant can sell or give away his or her share to someone else. So on death, a tenant in common's share in the property goes according to that person's will or if there is not a will, according to the distribution set out by the laws of intestacy (dying without a will.)

To use some cottage-related examples of these two methods of ownership, imagine that you leave your cottage in your will to your two children in joint tenancy. When the first of them dies, the surviving child (and, later, likely his or her spouse or children) will get the whole cottage. In situations where this happens, the grandchildren of the cottage owner whose parent died first may very well wonder why their cousins got the cottage and they didn't. In effect the winner is the family of the cottage owner's child who outlives his or her sibling.

In a tenancy in common situation, when the first child dies, that child's share in the property is distributed according to his or her will and if there is not a will, according to the intestacy distribution. So, if that child leaves his or her share in the cottage to his or her spouse, that may feel like a better solution, but of course then the original cottage owner's child (or children) is sharing the cottage with a sister-in-law or a brother-in-law. That outcome may be a perfectly workable solution—or it may be a disaster.

No matter what happens, allowing the transfer of the family cottage to be determined by which child dies first is, you have to admit, a little random.

disagreements over use and maintenance

Another issue that commonly comes up in the transfer of the cottage to the next generation is: who really wants the place? Or more to the point: who is prepared to spend time there and look after the place in the same way that it has always been cared for? And this question of tangible commitment involves not only time spent but also significant expenses, including property tax, and the required upkeep and renovations.

taxes

The potential for a daunting capital gains tax bill can tend to overshadow the entire family-cottage-transfer discussion, resulting in the other more subjective issues we've mentioned being ignored. While we don't think it is smart to overlook these less tangible issues, nevertheless you can't cook up a way to transfer the cottage down the family tree without getting tax advice.

How much capital gains tax will be payable and when will it arise? Can it be deferred? How do the various options for transferring the cottage compare in terms of the tax consequences? The creation of a big capital gains tax bill is a possibility whenever a so-called capital property that is not your main home or subject to some type of exemption is sold. As we say, you need professional advice, based not only on the characteristics of the property but also on your overall income tax situation.

ideas to consider

In planning for your family's cottage transfer, try to balance the hard-numbers issues (capital gains tax, property tax, maintenance and upkeep expenses) with the more subjective questions, such as the schedule of usage of the property and who will actually be in charge of making sure the work gets done. Other tough questions include what happens when one of the kids gets divorced, has financial problems, wants to get out of the property or dies.

A good solution for you and your family likely starts with a number of open-ended, casual discussions where people say what they think without having it all nailed down immediately, then moves to discussions with a professional (an estate lawyer or a tax accountant) to talk about how to achieve the family's intentions. Possibilities that he or she may suggest include:

- a sale to one of the children at fair market value now

- a transfer at death to one of the children at fair market value, representing part of that child's equal share of the estate

- transferring the property now into the children's names if the children can agree on a cohabitation agreement

- transferring the property to the children as tenants in common under the will but only if they can agree on the terms of a tenancy-in-common agreement; failing that agreement, the property will be sold

- insurance planning to address potential taxes on death of the owner(s)

An estate mediator told us she does her best family-cottage work if the family comes to see her before the cottage conversation gets really heated. If she is called in when the situation has fallen apart, years may have passed and perhaps litigation has been started. Most often this occurs when the children learn about the cottage's disposition in the will at the worst possible time: after the death of their last surviving parent. With too much coming at them, including the transfer of the cottage in some unexpected fashion, conflict can start in even the most amicable family.

As we said at the outset, the family cottage refuses to be simply relegated to the status of an asset; if you own one and have had it for a number of years, think about engaging your family in a discussion about how to make its transfer to the next generation in a mature and effective way. Who knows? The best solution of all may turn out to be one of your kids buying the Rolling Rock for fair market value and throwing an annual cottage reunion for old time's sake.

points to take away

▶ Start early as a family to sort out the cottage's future.

▶ Avoid transferring your cottage to your children in a way that may lead to unintended consequences in the future. It's better to do the planning and scenario forecasting early—and with your children—so that your children (and their children) do not become victims of the method of legal ownership that you put in your will.

▶ It is one thing for everyone to say "in theory" that they sure do want to continue to use the family cottage; it is quite another to put time, energy and money into a place that may be all the way across the country from where one or more of the kids now lives.

▶ The payment of tax on a family cottage is a very important consideration when you contemplate its sale or transfer to a trust, to strangers or to your children, either during your life or at your death. Insurance planning to address this possibility may be suggested by your advisors.

▶ It is a mistake to simply transfer your cottage by using a clause in your will, without consulting your family about options. Doing so strips away the chance for your kids to express their interest (or not) in the cottage, and it also adds an unnecessary element of chance or luck to the cottage's future ownership.

"... AND THOSE OF MY OFFICE PLANTS ALIVE AT MY DEATH TO MY PARTNER, HUGH, FOR HIS OWN USE ABSOLUTELY"

MISTAKE #32

Inadequately planning for the distribution of your personal effects

YOU MAY THINK NO ONE WILL WANT your accordion, the one you have played at every family gathering for the last 40 years. Sure, maybe they won't (we wouldn't, thanks) but then again, lawsuits have been started over Dad's lucky socks and his harmonica. So the mistake we are talking about here is underestimating just how important it can be to focus on the distribution of your "stuff," that is, personal effects such as art, jewellery and antiques.

In thinking about the best way to deal with personal effects in a will, we are reminded of the story "Goldilocks and the Three Bears." Just as Goldilocks found the porridge too hot, then too cold and then just right, you need to find the perfect balance between being overly specific in your will about your personal possessions and not planning for their distribution at all.

Like so many aspects of will planning, the right balance is highly dependent on your own situation. The factors to consider include the type of personal property that you own, whether anyone in your circle is overtly interested or uninterested in receiving any of it, your attachment to the items, your desire for an orderly distribution of personal effects at your death and the dynamics of your own circle of loved ones.

Here are three ways to think about distributing your personal property at your death:

1. a general transfer

This approach involves a paragraph in your will describing personal effects in a general way, such as "all articles of personal and household use or ornament and all automobiles and their accessories." The effect of a paragraph like this is to completely (no strings attached) transfer all of your personal property to one person, often your main beneficiary such as your spouse. The paragraph can then also *suggest* that the recipient may choose to give one, some or all of the items to other people, as he or she sees fit. Essentially this type of provision means that the articles are a *gift* to the named person and any further distribution by that person is discretionary; in other words, there is no obligation for him or her to do anything further. A variation of this type of will provision is to transfer all your personal property to your executor, to be distributed as he or she sees fit, or to sell the items and add the proceeds to the value of your estate available for distribution.

2. a general transfer with the possibilty of a memorandum made later

This is Option #1 but with an additional reference to a list or memorandum that you will "leave at your death" that you hope will be read and followed. This approach is still discretionary for the named recipient or your executor; he or she can choose to ignore the list or memorandum, because it is not part of the will.

3. specific gifts

With this approach, you describe each item and the recipient. These provisions are binding on your executor; occasionally if there are a number of different items gifted in this way, the list is attached as an appendix to the will but it is *still a binding part of the will* because it is prepared and attached before the will is signed.

One of our messages throughout the book is to approach your will planning as if it is indeed going to be your "last will." It may sound silly to suggest that people do something called a "last will" not really thinking that it will be the last, but many problems in estate administration, including acrimony over the distribution of personal effects, arise because people were a little too cavalier about their estate planning with the end result that their intentions simply were not stipulated.

In Jean's experience, and that of estate lawyers with whom we spoke, most couples doing their will planning together use the "all to my spouse" personal effects clause and then rely on Option #2 above, referring to a personal effects memorandum that will be written up sometime between the date of the will and their death. Single people often simply go straight to Option #2, requesting that their executor distribute the effects according to the memorandum that will be prepared sometime in the future.

Hmm . . .

Have you ever asked someone what he or she is doing on the weekend and heard the answer, "Oh, my husband and I are working on our personal effects memorandum"?

No, you haven't.

You may have been told that your friend or colleague is cleaning the garage, whacking the weeds or competing in the Ironman, but rest assured no one has ever claimed to be doing their personal effects memorandum. These often-mentioned documents rarely, if ever, get done.

So the moral of the story is, if you have one or more articles of personal property that you really do want to go to someone, like your Olympic medals, then you would be wise to state that specifically in your will à la Option #3 above.

Or, you can defy the odds and prepare a memorandum which, if really completed, has the advantage of being a document that you can update as you acquire new items of importance or as you give away or sell items that were on your original memo. As we mentioned above under Option #2, such a memorandum is not legally binding because it does not form part of the will, but it is very likely that directions and wishes stated in writing by you will be taken seriously and will be followed. The trick is to actually get the memorandum done. Then you should ideally store it along with the original will.

Before we leave this topic, one item to note is that personal effects provisions are especially important in relationships where the bulk of the estate will be going to people *other than the surviving partner*. For example, let's say you are in a second marriage and each of you has a will leaving your assets (which you have mostly kept separate) to the children of your first marriages. That sounds fine, but as part of your plan for continuity after the first death, you may assume that personal property will remain with the surviving spouse. Sad to say, but more than one trust professional we spoke with mentioned situations where the children of the deceased spouse descended on the home to claim personal property that they declared to be part of their late mom's or dad's estate. In short, even if you do want your children from your first marriage to receive all or most of your financial worth, be clear about what should happen to the personal effects that you and your second spouse use and enjoy in your daily lives.

points to take away

▶ The distribution of personal property, even items of little or no monetary value, can cause a lot of bickering and conflict at our death.

▶ There are several ways to deal with personal property in our will, including: leaving it all to the discretion of our executor or someone else; leaving a non-binding memorandum; or making specific and binding gifts of personal items right in our will.

▶ If items are important to you, be sure to state right in your will where they should go or use a non-binding memorandum referred to in your will. Get that memorandum done within a reasonable time, and store it where it will be found by your executor, preferably with the original will.

THE SOCIETY OF WAYWARD PETS AND OTHER CAUSES CLOSE TO YOUR HEART

MISTAKE #33

Not taking full advantage of the opportunity to make a difference in the world through charitable giving

ALMOST ALWAYS, ESTATE PLANNING has an air of getting your affairs in order and disposing of your assets in a transactional way. But people who decide to include charitable giving as part of the exercise often find they open the door to reflecting on their life and what has mattered to them in the community. Regardless of the size of the gifts you leave to charity in your will, your legacy can make the largest difference if you take some time with the process rather than simply telling your lawyer which charities to include in, say, paragraph 5(d) of the will.

Thoughtfully done, charitable giving refers to a process of giving money or assets to a charitable organization in the way that makes the most sense to both the donor and the charity, either while the donor is alive or after death. It involves a careful consideration of many questions and ideas: life insurance options, cash bequests or gifts of property, the tax ramifications, and whether you want to give to a charitable organization that does charitable work directly or a foundation whose primary focus is to financially support people and organizations working directly for the cause in question.

(When we refer here to a *charitable organization*, we mean a charity or public or private foundation registered with the federal government and thus able to issue tax receipts. Of course you can give your money to any organization you want—your kid's ball team, your poker group—but only registered charitable organizations are subject to stringent oversight by the Canadian government, qualify for special tax treatment as a charity and are able to give a tax receipt.)

As technically complicated as charitable giving (sometimes called *planned giving*) can be, problems with the technicalities was not the most common refrain we heard when talking to professionals in the charitable sector. The most frequently given advice was to *speak with the charitable organizations and your family in advance of finalizing your plans*. By doing so, you will be able to:

- Get to know the charitable organizations well and understand their mission statements. Many charities have two or three charitable purposes, such as conducting research in the hope of ending a disease *and* providing financial support to people diagnosed with the disease. You may prefer that your money go to one of such objectives over the others.

- Understand the various methods for benefiting the community through your gift. For example, if there is a community foundation in your area such as The Calgary Foundation or The Halifax Foundation, their experienced professionals can help you better understand the different ways that your gift can be used to make the most lasting impact in the community.

- Have an easy way to start conversations among your loved ones about your charitable intentions and to assess who in your family may want to be involved after you are gone in carrying out your personal legacy; and

- Work in a relaxed manner (not in a mad frenzy as you are preparing your will before a big trip) with your professional advisors about the different options to consider, from giving cash now to donating securities now or at your death. There are numerous ways to give to charities from the perspective of both tax relief and achieving your personal goals.

Early communication with charities means that you can learn from their professionals about the best way to achieve your goals. For example, if you are planning to leave a gift in an endowed fund, meaning the gift will be invested and used in perpetuity, then you will want to think in a visionary manner: those causes that are a priority now can change in the years ahead. Diseases evolve from deadly killers to manageable chronic illnesses; efforts to improve urban environments have broadened over recent years from simply parks to downtown rooftops. *Gifts specifically fixed on one goal to be achieved in only one way can lose the innovative edge that the donor likely desired when he or she envisioned the difference the gift would make.*

If you speak in advance with a charity, their professionals can alert you to the ways that flexibility can be built into an endowed fund that you set up now or through your will, avoiding uncertainty, guesswork or even a court application to get advice and directions on the right thing to do with the funds to carry out your intentions. Especially for a sizable gift, a charity is best able to maximize the gift's value if its representatives are able to plan alongside the donor, by learning about the donor's values and goals. As well, if the charity is a small organization, giving it the chance to prepare for the receipt of a significant gift can make a world of difference in its ability to use the gift most effectively.

Even gifts on a smaller scale can be immeasurably enhanced if you talk to the charity first. One lawyer shared with us the story of a client who wanted to leave a gift to a charity that operated small vans for handicapped people and seniors. The client asked that the gift be drafted to include not only the purchase of a van but also ongoing maintenance and repairs. However, in speaking with the charity, the lawyer learned it could absolutely not accept gifts for repairs because, for whatever reason, upkeep and repairs were a responsibility of the municipal government. Simply writing the client's original idea into the will would have resulted, at her death, in her executor spending extra time and professional fees to sort out the appropriate approach, with possibly a court application being required.

When it comes to communicating with family members, many people assume that what matters to them will also matter to their children, but that kind of thinking is a little outdated. Charities prefer not to be placed in the awkward situation of working with family members who are indifferent to their late parent's cause or, worse, downright angry at the gift being made at all.

Communication with your loved ones throughout your life about your philanthropic intentions will result in a much greater chance that your objectives will be achieved. Maybe you will be disappointed to find that your children aren't in fact interested in your favourite causes, but you may be delighted to discover that you are interested in *their* philanthropic concerns and can thus choose to leave a legacy to something that really matters to *them*. There's little to be gained from trying to "control from the grave" because usually that approach doesn't work too well over the long term.

The best and most long-lasting approach for charitable giving in your will is to develop a relationship with the charities and to have the conversation (or many!) with your professional advisors and family. Times change, causes change, people change, and the more vision and flexibility you bring to charitable giving, the more impact you will achieve whether your gift is $1,000 or $1,000,000.

points to take away

▶ There are many ways in which you can benefit charities during your life and after your death. Some are complicated and involve complex tax planning and others are more straightforward.

▶ Professionals at charities and foundations do their best work for a donor when they have the chance to get to know both the person and his or her philanthropic intentions. Getting some advice from the charities you wish to include in your will and from your tax advisor and lawyer makes a lot of sense.

▶ It also makes sense to talk to your family. Discussions about philanthropic intentions can be started early; you never know what you will find out and how your philanthropic plans can be shaped in a way that interests your family. Control from the grave is really no control at all.

THE STONY PASTURE AND OTHER PLACES NOT ON THE MAP

MISTAKE #34

Not paying enough attention to the ownership and description of your assets

IT'S A COMMON MISTAKE for people to be a little light in their knowledge about the legal descriptions of their property, and sometimes we can even be mistaken about whether we own an asset at all. As you might expect, these problems can lead to even bigger issues in our estate planning.

those confusing legal descriptions

Once when Jean was around the age of six or seven, she and her dad were driving around a pasture quite a ways from the actual farm, only to wind up with the car perched on a large boulder, see-sawing back and forth. It was quite traumatic at the time—to Jean, not her dad—and from then on, the family called that piece of land "the Stony Pasture." You won't find the Stony Pasture on any municipal map of Saskatchewan, just as you won't find your own family's Rolling River cottage described that way—but you'd be surprised by how many people use only a vague, inaccurate or colloquial description to identify property in their wills.

Mistakes in wills make up a whole class in law school . . . okay, not quite a whole class, but there is a textbook with that very name, *Mistakes in Wills*, and it is often referred to in court cases dealing with, yes, mistakes in wills.

One case out of New Brunswick considered an argument over a legal description that included a parcel's identifying number and then in brackets were the pesky words, "200 acres more or less." We say "pesky" because the property was really only 121 acres, *not* 200 acres, and if you think fighting over 79 acres seems like a waste of time, be assured that people can fight over a deceased person's picture frames if they set their minds to it.

The law about mistakes in wills is complicated and at the risk of oversimplifying it, one important principle is that Canadian courts are reluctant to accept evidence about what the deceased person "really meant." A court would prefer to review the will "on its face" and decide from there what was intended rather than start to accept conjecture about who said what to whom during the deceased's lifetime.

With that general principle in mind, in the New Brunswick case the judge said that the property number was clear and that the words in brackets about the acreage could be ignored as "surplus or inessential." However, the point here is not how far you can go with vague legal descriptions; the point is that you need to nail down accurate descriptions of your property. Also ask yourself if it is necessary to refer to specific property at all: sometimes people fall into the trap of describing and giving away each asset separately in their will, each parcel of land and each bank account. The problem is that we tend to gather new assets as life goes on and dispose of other assets, and it is impractical to think that we can keep updating our wills at the same pace.

If there is a specific item that you really want to give to a specific person, then be sure to describe it accurately and legally, and be sure to update your will if you sell or give the item away or the named recipient dies.

giving away items you don't own

One of the earliest notions a toddler grasps is ownership; you can test this theory by taking away an item that a three-year-old believes to be his or hers. "MINE!!" comes the outraged cry. As we grow up and both our relationships and our possessions get more complicated, what we own can get confusing, leading to the possibility of big mistakes in our wills.

Different forms of legal ownership exist for a number of reasons such as tax effectiveness, risk management and the limitation of liability. The actual form of legal ownership may often slip our minds because if we use or enjoy an asset it becomes easy to think that it is "ours"—and legally ours to give away.

As an example, let's say that you have a beautiful Group of Seven painting in your office. You love this painting—in fact you picked it out yourself years ago. But let's add the twist that you are one of three shareholders in a small business, and all of the art was bought by the company and is a corporate asset. This means that even though you consider your Lawren Harris painting to be yours, it isn't, and it cannot be given away by you, while you are alive or through your will. You can direct that all or some of your *shares* in the business go to certain people in your will (subject to sound tax-planning advice), but that is quite a bit different than leaving "your" beloved painting to your spouse.

Another good example of giving away what we don't have is trying to give away real estate or a bank account that is held with another person in joint tenancy. Our interest in property held in joint tenancy goes to the surviving joint tenant when we die, subject to our comments in Mistakes #8 and #9 about joint tenancies between parents and adult children. So, if you own the family farm in joint tenancy with your brother, you may think about leaving your share to your spouse in your will, but that won't be possible: your brother as the surviving joint tenant will automatically receive your interest in the family farm and it won't even form part of your estate.

If you are thinking, *What the heck . . . ?* keep in mind that in order to leave an interest in land or a bank account to someone in your will, you must either own the asset outright in your own name or hold your interest in it as a tenant in common. As mentioned in Mistake #31 in the cottage discussion, property held as a tenant in common means that you have an interest in the property that you can give away or sell during your lifetime or give away in your will. In contrast, you cannot give away by your will or before you die an interest in a property that you hold with someone else in joint tenancy. Confusing? Yes! Essential to understand it as you do your estate planning? Absolutely!

points to take away

▶ Before you start your estate planning, you need to have an iron grip on what you own and how your property is legally described.

▶ A will is your final statement of your intentions about who will receive everything you own at the time of your death; it pays to give close attention to exactly what it is that you own and if your method of ownership actually permits you to give away your interest in the property in your will.

YOU CAN'T GIVE WHAT YOU AIN'T GOT!

MISTAKE #35
Not paying enough attention to describing the gifts in your will appropriately

THERE ARE A LOT OF DIFFERENT SKILLS needed for good estate planning. These include math, a little economic forecasting, and, most of all, the sense to know that our financial picture the day we sign our wills may be quite a lot different than it is the day we die. The increase or decrease in our net worth between signing wills and passing away must be kept top of mind as we plan who gets what in our estates.

giving away more than 100 percent of the estate's value

We really do understand that professional hockey players can "dig down deep" and give "110 percent" in a big game, but the rest of us are stuck with having only 100 percent of anything, and so we need to keep an eye on how the shares of our estate are adding up as we sit down to plan our will.

One lawyer with years of experience in estate planning told us that she sees people "on a daily basis" try to give away more than they have. They arrive at the will-planning meeting armed with their lists of who gets what

percentage and who gets what if some or all of the first named beneficiaries predecease them, and, lo and behold, on careful analysis it adds up to
more than 100 percent if certain scenarios occur.

The same lawyer recommends the flow chart method of mapping out
visually all of the various beneficiaries and their shares, which reduces the
chance of giving away too much or too little. Giving away too much means
that your estate is going to spend some time in mediation or court as everyone tries to figure out your intention by looking at the will's wording. And
giving away too little is also bad because the remaining assets will need to
be distributed as if you died without a will—an undesirable result as we
discussed at length in Part 2.

ending up with an unintended result

Cash gifts are easy for your executor to figure out and pay—if a gift of
$10,000 is to be paid out, that is pretty straightforward and everyone, your
beneficiaries included, will know exactly how much they will receive once
the estate is ready to be distributed. On the other hand, in a recessionary
time, cash gifts can wind up being disproportionately large.

Here's an example:

Gillian's net worth was $1,400,000 when she signed her will at the age
of 75. The economy was vibrant, her investment portfolio had just nudged
over a million dollars and her downtown condominium in Calgary had
increased in value from $350,000 to $400,000 over the past year.

Gillian wanted her only son, Harold, to receive about $750,000 from
her estate and she fully expected to see her net worth continue to rise until
her death. Gillian enjoyed vibrant good health.

Thinking along these lines, Gillian included in her will some significant cash bequests—to her sisters, to several favourite charities and to two
neighbours—totalling $600,000. At the time she prepared her will, after the
payment of these gifts and the estimated taxes on the portfolio, the remain-
der in the estate going to Harold would have been about $750,000, exactly
the amount Gillian had in mind.

Unfortunately, two years after her will was prepared, Gillian suddenly
became ill and the economy entered a severe recession. When Gillian died

six months later, her investment portfolio was reduced to $750,000 and the value of her condo to $275,000. The taxes on her portfolio were of course lower due to the reduced value of her investments, but the stated cash gifts in the will were exactly as they had always been: $600,000.

Now the math didn't work out so well for Harold, because cash gifts are paid out before the balance is paid. After payment of cash gifts in the amount of $600,000, the balance of the estate was $475,000, not nearly what Harold's mother had intended to leave for him. If Gillian had considered the possible interplay between the specific cash bequests and the value of her estate, she would have considered using percentages for the gifts to sisters, friends and charities to ensure that no matter what happened in the economy her son would have received the lion's share of her estate.

points to take away

▶ Giving away more or less than the entirety of an estate happens more often than you might think. Use a flow chart to walk through each of the scenarios set out in your will to be sure that once all the portions are distributed there is neither a positive nor a negative balance.

▶ In providing for substantial cash gifts, think through the possible scenarios that may have an impact on your net worth. Ask yourself whether the cash gifts will still make sense if your estate suffers a serious drop in value. Speak with your lawyer about ways in which your will can be drafted so that your overall intentions will be carried out regardless of significant changes in the net worth of your estate.

CANADA REVENUE WHO?

MISTAKE #36

Making errors that may result in additional taxation of your estate

AS WE SPOKE WITH ESTATE-PLANNING PROFESSIONALS, four relatively straightforward tax-related mistakes kept coming up. The common theme in each of these four errors is that they are entirely avoidable with the advice of a competent advisor, but it is definitely worth your time to understand the points yourself. Equipped with an awareness of these issues, you'll be sure to share with your advisors all of the information needed to avoid these common planning bloopers:

- not contemplating the significant tax burden that may accrue on an asset over many years of ownership;

- giving assets to specific beneficiaries and being unclear about who pays the related taxes;

- missing the available planning techniques that defer taxation until the last spouse dies; and

- not addressing the ownership of foreign property or the foreign citizenship of the person preparing the will, a beneficiary of the will, or the spouse of a beneficiary.

not contemplating the significant tax burden that may accrue on an asset over many years of ownership

This point may sound too obvious to even mention but it is a "miss" in a lot of estate planning. Lurking among some people's assets may be a building or even a business that was bought or started 40 or 50 years ago. Sometimes the only discussion about it, even with the advisor, is that when the first spouse dies, the taxes will be deferred until the death of the last spouse to die. If no further thought is given to it until the person's death (or the last spouse's death), the tax bill can be staggering.

This can throw off the plan for a couple of reasons. First and most simply, since the tax wasn't properly considered, the person's estate can wind up leaving far less to the beneficiaries than he or she had planned. Second, if the idea is to pass on the asset rather than sell it, a provision in the will directing that to happen may not be possible if the estate is not able to pay the taxes from other estate funds. In that scenario, the asset would need to be sold to cover the taxes.

This point provides a perfect segue into the next one, which is . . .

giving assets to specific beneficiaries and being unclear about who pays the related taxes

In the prior point, we mentioned that sometimes people just don't think about the taxes that may be payable on an asset that has gone up in value. An additional problem arises if the asset is specified in the will as going to a particular beneficiary and the tax treatment (i.e., who will be responsible to pay the tax?) is not clear.

For example, if a farming couple has two significant assets, their homestead property and a registered retirement savings plan, both assets will most likely have a tax bill associated with them when the last spouse dies. Who is to pay that tax? What will be left "net" to each child after the taxes? How is the RRSP going to be directed to the child who will receive it—through the will or by a direct designation on the plan? The answers to these questions and others will determine if the two children are treated equally or not by their parent's will.

The solution is not to get out the calculator and the *Income Tax Act* when you and your advisor sit down to prepare your will. Between the date of your will and your death, chances are good that the *Tax Act* will change, in terms of both its application of tax and also the available exemptions, and so will the value of the assets. Far better to have your will drafted in a way that ensures equality of the beneficiaries on an after-tax basis, assuming equality is your intention. Your intention may not be equality on a value basis; your intention may simply be that you want certain beneficiaries to receive specific assets. *Great.* You still need to address the basic question of who is going to be responsible for the tax.

There is no right answer because it all depends on what you are trying to achieve. If you want a certain niece to get a parcel of land she has always loved and that is her entire gift, then likely your desired approach is that the estate pays any capital gains tax arising on the land rather than make your niece responsible for the tax owing before she can receive the gift. On the other hand, if your goal is to attain an equal (value-wise) distribution among a group of beneficiaries, such as your children, then your advisor may recommend dividing the entire "residue" equally among that group. If one of the beneficiaries really wants a particular asset in the estate, then that can be arranged on a fair market value but in a way that ensures that equal distribution takes place.

Your advisor will have solutions for any issue that you raise or distribution that you want to discuss; our point is to make sure that these issues are raised and discussed.

missing the available planning techniques that defer taxation until the last spouse dies

Leaving everything you own to your spouse or partner is the most common estate plan going and lines up nicely with the law's requirement that people look after people who depend on them financially. Further, and perhaps most important, you can take advantage of a tax deferral that is available in Canada, often called a *spousal rollover*, which allows you to roll your assets to your spouse and defer the payment of tax on those assets until your spouse's death.

However, for one reason or another, sometimes a will leaves an asset to someone other than the deceased's spouse and the result is that the taxes on the asset end up being paid earlier than need be. If this is being done with full intention and awareness of the tax consequences, that is fine, but usually when this happens in an estate, everyone involved suspects that it was a mistake.

The most common occurrence of this is when a parent leaves his or her registered retirement savings plan (RRSP) to an adult child instead of to the surviving spouse. This can be done by naming the child directly as the plan's beneficiary on the plan itself, or by a separate clause in the will. Either way, because the RRSP is not being rolled over to a surviving spouse, the taxes payable arise at the first spouse's death rather than the last spouse's death. As well, unless the will says otherwise, the tax on the RRSPs is payable by the estate and this may leave the surviving spouse strapped for cash at a time when he or she needs money the most.

Not all assets have a lurking tax bill waiting to be paid. For example, if you leave an adult child a gift of $10,000 in cash or your fishing equipment, no tax would be payable. On cash, you have already paid the tax, and most personal effects do not appreciate significantly after we buy them.

The point is, be good and sure that you don't leave someone who isn't your spouse an asset that will create a premature tax bill in the estate. If you do want to do this, at least do it *knowing* the tax consequences.

not addressing foreign ownership or foreign citizenship of the person preparing the will, a beneficiary or a beneficiary's spouse

When speaking to estate lawyers and tax accountants, we heard about these problems a lot! Somehow the foreign citizenship of a person preparing a will or the foreign citizenship of a beneficiary can get glossed over in the estate-planning process, so that the relevant planning for these factors is neglected. Or, perhaps even more commonly, Canadians buy foreign real estate with the same approach as they buy Canadian real estate (with a casual purchase and sale agreement, maybe a mortgage), not realizing that professional advice is required on how to best hold the property from a tax and will-planning perspective.

As one chartered accountant put it, people buy and sell Canadian real estate all the time and don't think too much about how they do it or the tax impact of it. But when it comes to buying real estate outside of Canada, the stakes are higher, and before you buy foreign property you really need to get professional advice on how to do it.

Buying foreign property, particularly real estate, means that you will be affected by the tax regime of not one country but two: as Canadian residents, we are assessed tax on our "worldwide income," but the country where we own the property may also tax us due to our ownership of property within their borders.

For example, the estate taxes applicable to American citizens *and* to citizens of other countries who own American property are both complicated and constantly evolving. But although we most often think about foreign property ownership as the homes owned by Canadian snowbirds from Florida to California, advisors spoke often about the diversity of Canadians' foreign property ownership. Whether the property is in Naples, Florida or Paris the advice is the same: run—don't walk—to an advisor with cross-border experience to determine if:

- the way you are holding the property makes sense;
- your will adequately addresses the treatment of the foreign property at your death; and
- your will needs to be reviewed by a lawyer in the foreign country.

The last point about the will being reviewed by a lawyer in the country where the property is located can be extremely important. It is important to understand the other country's laws on matters such as who can inherit and in what manner, how a valid will is prepared, witnessed and signed, and who can be an executor. A clear understanding of these concepts helps to ensure the desired distribution of your property in that country upon your death.

Trust officers spoke to us about having the experience of sending good, solid Canadian wills over to other countries where the deceased person had owned property, only to be told that the will or its contents were invalid. Roadblocks like that in an estate administration can cost the estate months of time and thousands of dollars in legal fees.

points to take away

▶ Tax-related mistakes in estate planning usually happen when a person attempts a "creative" approach, such as leaving specific assets to certain people. This can result in the early payment of tax because the option of using a spousal rollover is lost and it can create ambiguity as to who is to pay the taxes.

▶ Start with a clear idea of your goals (equality; certain assets to certain people; sufficient cash in the estate to pay the tax) and then be sure your estate lawyer knows your goals and is fully aware of all of your assets, how their ownership is held by you and where the assets are located.

▶ If you or your loved ones are foreign citizens, just because you are also a Canadian resident will likely not change the impact of the foreign country's laws on your estate. Start with your own advisor and consider the involvement of a lawyer in the other country as well.

▶ The method of ownership of foreign property is critical. The most important times to get advice are when the property is being bought and when the will is being prepared. If you purchase foreign property without advice and own it in your own name, in joint tenancy, in a corporation or in a trust, you may end up needing to unravel the method of ownership at the time you prepare your will when the tax implications are reviewed.

CAN I HAVE A SILVER SPOON WITH THAT?

MISTAKE #37

Misunderstanding trusts in general and mistakes in the trustee selection

A TRUST IS A FAIRLY SIMPLE CONCEPT but it is easy to make mistakes in using it in wills. If an estate lawyer has a whiteboard at hand and gets going on a discussion about what a trust is, he or she will often draw a triangle as the symbol for a trust because a trust has three essential parts:

- the *settlor*: the source of the trust assets;
- the *trustee*: the person or trust company holding the trust assets; and
- the *beneficiaries*: the persons intended to benefit from the trust assets.

The most common mistakes when it comes to trusts set up in people's wills are in (1) the appointment of the trustee; and (2) the terms of the distribution of the funds to the beneficiaries. In this mistake we will discuss possible pitfalls in the trustee selection and in Mistake #38 the common errors that arise in setting out the trust's terms for distribution.

mistakes in the selection of the trustee

You often hear the phrase, "executor and trustee." These are actually two separate roles, requiring the appointed person to wear two hats. The executor duties involve the administration of the estate from the date of death until the distribution of the assets. This distribution may include flowing some or all of the estate assets into one or more trusts. The executor then switches hats and becomes the trustee of the trust or trusts. The trustee duties involve the administration and operation of the trust for the benefit of the beneficiaries, carried out according to the terms of the will.

In other cases, the executor of the estate and the trustee of one or more of the will's trusts are different people.

conflict of interest in acting as both trustee and guardian

Many people know only a few people whom they would trust to carry out the estate administration, act as the guardian of their minor children, or be the trustee of their children's money. The result may be that the same person is asked to carry out two or three of these roles. However, it is worth thinking carefully about whether multiple tasks may result in a situation where the appointed person's interests are potentially in conflict. For example, if the guardian of your young children is also the trustee of the funds for your children and he or she is also raising children of his or her own, there may be a financial disparity between your children's trust fund and the guardian and trustee's own financial situation.

In one situation, the guardians and the trustees of minor children (who had lost their parents early in life) were the same people, a couple with children of their own who had been close friends of the deceased parents. They used money from the bereaved children's trust to make a large addition to their own home. Ostensibly this was done because their home was too small to take in the additional children when the children's parents died. This may have been a sound decision—but the relatives of the children disagreed and successfully applied to the court to have a trust company replace the couple as the trustees. It appeared to the court and to the trust company that the house addition was more favourable to the long-term value of the guardian's home than to the long-term benefit of the orphaned minors. It was still unclear whether the deceased parents' children would later be compensated for the expenditure unwisely made by the guardians.

conflict of interest between trustee and beneficiary

A trustee can also have a conflict of interest with one or more of the beneficiaries of the trust. To understand this concept, think of trust beneficiaries as being in one or both of two categories:

1. life beneficiaries receiving income or capital, and sometimes both income and capital, from the trust during all or part of their lifetimes; and

2. capital beneficiaries receiving the capital remaining in the trust when a certain event occurs, such as the death of one or more of the lifetime beneficiaries mentioned in #1.

A trust is sometimes used in a second marriage situation, where a trust is set up for the surviving spouse from the second marriage for his or her lifetime, and when the surviving spouse dies, the balance in the trust is paid to the children from the first marriage. In this scenario, if either the surviving spouse or a child of the first marriage is a trustee, there is inherently a conflict between that trustee's personal interests and the role of a trustee. This is because every dollar spent during the surviving spouse's lifetime means less is left over for the children of the first marriage. You can see why it is important to pay attention to who is the trustee in this situation: the trust is intended to look after the surviving second spouse but also to preserve assets for the children from the first marriage. In setting up a trust like this in a will, think long and hard about whether the surviving second spouse or any of the children from the first marriage should be the trustee.

It is in these situations that people often think about a trust company or an impartial, independent friend or advisor to be the trustee. It doesn't take a lot of imagination to think of the disputes that can and do arise. Let's say that the surviving second spouse, Harry, has a source of income other than the trust left in the will of his late wife, Sally. Harry's stepchildren (who will receive the balance of the trust when he dies) may believe that those separate funds should be used for living expenses rather than look to the trust set up by their mother Sally's will. On the other hand, Harry's children from *his* first marriage (who will be receiving the balance of Harry's estate at his death) may prefer that Harry look to the trust funds rather than deplete his own wealth.

We hasten to say that we are simply raising red flags to consider here; we are not advocating mistrust of everyone whom you love and care about. There are no black and white decrees that must or even should be followed in every case. There are situations where stepchildren are much kinder to their elderly stepmom than her own kids, and other cases where stepchildren begrudge every cent paid to the step-parent from their late parent's will. The key is to be aware of situations that *may* create challenges and have occasionally been a problem in others' estates, and then assess your own family dynamics against this knowledge.

points to take away

▶ Trusts in wills are very useful estate-planning tools. Common uses include ensuring that our minor children are cared for if we die when they are young or that others we love are provided for after our death.

▶ Every situation is unique, but pay attention to the selection of your trustee. If there is a conflict of interest inherent in the appointment, you should discuss this with your lawyer. The conflict of interest may not disqualify that individual from acting as your trustee, but it is worth considering alternatives, including the appointment of an independent and objective trustee, such as a trustworthy individual outside of the family circle or a trust company.

CAN I HAVE A SILVER SPOON WITH THAT? THE SEQUEL

 MISTAKE #38

Making mistakes in setting out the terms of the trusts in the will

THE MOST COMMON MISTAKES in trusts set up in people's wills are the selection of trustee and the directions for distributing assets out of the trust for the beneficiaries. In Mistake #37, we discussed the selection of the trustee and here we will talk about that second category—mistakes that come up in setting out the trust's provisions for distribution.

trusts for minor children

In a trust for minor children, ideally the will balances specific directions about what the money is to be used for while still allowing the trustee some flexibility to deal with new issues that arise. The younger your children are when you prepare your will, the more flexibility you should build into the terms. Children's needs at an age of complete dependency will differ from their needs as they grow older. In planning for the unlikely possibility of dying when your children are young, an important principle to keep in mind is that your children's needs and interests could develop in many different and unexpected ways as they grow up, and you want the trust to be flexible enough to address these developments.

Having said that, a will is a formal legal document and it is not the place for parents to set out each and every factor that the trustee of the children's trust should consider. Your lawyer can provide suggested wording to allow your will to reflect your overall perspective on appropriate distributions from your children's trust while still providing the legal clarity and certainty needed in a will.

In addition, you could consider preparing an informal document which, although not binding on your trustee, will provide your trustee with more details of your thoughts and perspectives on how to use the trust for the benefit of your children. Just be sure to prepare any such document with your lawyer's guidance and before your will is finalized; your informal musings need to be aligned with the crisp language of the will or you run the risk of your intentions being unclear.

Trusts in wills for minor children commonly direct the trustee to invest a certain lump sum of money comprising the trust and called the *capital* of the trust. Any interest earned on the lump sum is called the *income* of the trust. Income that is not spent right away is often added to the original lump sum and becomes capital. Distributions of funds from the trust are either *capital distributions*, as they are made from the capital of the trust, or *income distributions*, as they are made from the income of the trust.

Ultimately your children will grow up and receive the capital of the trust, so in addition to crafting the terms of how they are cared for while they are little, you need to contemplate the long-term distribution. A common approach to children receiving the capital distributions is where a specified portion is paid out at each of several stages such as at ages 21, 25 and 30. As well, the child may receive part or all of the income from the trust between those ages and additional lump sum payments in the exercise of the trustee's discretion, for example, for university tuition.

One approach that Jean likes is the income being paid out in its entirety at a certain age, such as at the age of majority, as a trial run on cash management. Your child may make some mistakes when that income starts to be paid, but squandering some income at age 18 or 19 is likely preferable to blowing the first capital distribution at the age of 21 or 25. As we have said throughout the book, there isn't a right answer to any of these issues because everyone is different when it comes to financial matters. There are the 10-year-old lemonade-stand owners who mysteriously accumulate several hundred dollars over a summer as well as the middle-aged high income earner with a lifestyle far exceeding his or her income. One size does not fit all in money matters or in planning wills.

spousal trusts

In Mistake #37, we discussed spousal trusts, sometimes used in the wills of people in second or subsequent marriages as a way to preserve assets for the children of earlier relationships. We discussed there the importance of thinking carefully about who should be the trustee in a spousal trust, but it is also essential to spend time on the terms for the distribution of income and capital to the spouse while he or she is alive.

One important consideration is whether the trust terms support your desired tax goals. Just as leaving assets directly to a surviving spouse can be a very tax-favourable approach in will planning, so can giving assets to a trust for a spouse. However, the *Income Tax Act* sets out clear rules as to how a spousal trust needs to be drafted to qualify for the favourable tax treatment. It is a common mistake to accidentally create a "tainted" spousal trust, the result of a poorly drafted trust in a will not complying with the *Income Tax Act*. Accordingly, be sure that your tax objectives are known to and discussed with your drafting lawyer.

In addition to thinking about taxes, if the purpose of the trust is primarily to look after the spouse, then the trust in the will needs to be drafted in a way in which that is made clear. There is a principle in trust law called the "even hand rule," which directs that in the administration of a trust, the trustee cannot favour one beneficiary over the other—unless the terms of the trust stipulate that one is to be favoured.

It is clearly important in setting up a spousal trust to review with your lawyer what your overall objectives are and how they can be achieved in the trust, keeping in mind the family dynamics, the expected size of your estate and the nature of the assets.

A good example of how the nature of the estate assets can impact a spousal trust involved a couple's home designated as a heritage property. The husband survived the wife, receiving the entire interest in this home as well as a lifetime interest in the rest of his late wife's estate. The terms of that spousal trust included the ability to encroach on the capital, which is really just a fancy way of saying that the capital could be used for ad hoc amounts as needed at the discretion of the trustee.

A challenging question arose for the trustee because the home had never been renovated and the renovation estimate for bringing this heritage property up to standards was a daunting amount. The terms of the trust were not clear on whether this type of encroachment on the trust's capital was what the wife had in mind, even though, with some advance thinking, repairs to a hundred-year-old home should have been expected and contemplated in the drafting of the will.

In this particular case, the deceased wife's children did *not* object to the payment of the renovations from the spousal trust, the balance of which would eventually go to them, with the renovated home going to their step-siblings. However, we can imagine other situations in which this type of encroachment would have been vehemently opposed.

In summary, when thinking about the terms of trusts in your will, you really need to put yourself into the situation as if it will happen tomorrow. Discuss the possible outcomes with your advisors, within the context of what you are trying to achieve.

points to take away

▶ One of the challenges with setting up trusts in your will is that none of us can rule from the grave and it is foolish to even try. However, it is important to think about your objectives in setting up the trust and also the outcomes that you want to achieve *and* want to avoid.

▶ You may want to consider ancillary informal documents that affirm the trusts set up in your will while adding further "flavour" to your intentions as a reference point for your trustee. It is imperative that any such documents be drawn up with your lawyer's advice and assistance to ensure that these documents do not contradict or confuse the intentions set out in your will.

▶ Balancing clarity with flexibility will require frank, in-depth discussions with your lawyer. If your will includes trusts for minor children, the terms of the trust need to cover both how your children's trust will be used for their benefit while they are young and also the ultimate distribution of capital to your children.

▶ Communicating the overall contents of your will to those who are affected is usually wise. This advice is especially pertinent if your will involves a trust for your spouse, the remaining capital of which will go to children from another marriage, or a trust for any other adult (such as a spendthrift child) who may question why their inheritance is being held in trust at all.

MINIMUM WAGE SOUNDS ABOUT RIGHT, MARGE

MISTAKE #39
Not planning ahead for the compensation of your executor

ETIQUETTE BOOKS SUGGEST we don't talk about certain topics in social chit-chat—subjects like religion, politics, sex and money are apparently off limits. While that is interesting, somehow talking about money can be challenging no matter how well we know others. Perhaps that is why people make the mistake of glossing over their executor's compensation in their will planning and it may also be why the law uses flowery and fairly unhelpful phrases in describing an executor's compensation. A phrase like "fair and reasonable allowance for the care, pains and trouble and the time expended" is usually found in any description of an executor's fee. What does that phrase tell you about paying your executor? Not a lot!

To avoid the mistake of not planning for your executor's compensation, you need to know the advantages and disadvantages of all of your options:

1. Say nothing about it in the will.

2. Specifically state that no compensation shall be paid.

3. Provide clearly for your executor's compensation in the will.

4. Leave a gift to the executor.

1. say nothing

If your will is silent on executor compensation, your executor is still entitled to claim a fee at the time that he or she asks the beneficiaries to approve the estate administration. This is also when the executor asks the beneficiaries to sign a release that releases the executor from liability in administering the estate up to that time. Typically the approval-and-release happens right before the beneficiaries receive the final distribution of their share of the estate.

Provincial legislation provides guidelines for the appropriate compensation of an executor and trustee, and there are also a number of court cases that provide direction as to how the guidelines should be applied. Those cases use language like the arcane phrase we mentioned above, highlighting the fact that each estate is unique, meaning that although the compensation needs to be within a reasonable range, it also can be much higher or lower depending on the work *actually done in administering this particular estate.*

Factors often referred to in an analysis of an executor's proposed fee include the:

1. magnitude of the estate;
2. care, responsibility and risks assumed by the executor;
3. time spent by the executor in carrying out his or her responsibilities;
4. skill and ability required and displayed by the executor; and
5. results obtained and degree of success associated with the efforts of the executor.

As suggested by these five factors, time-consuming and delicate challenges such as litigation, conflict among the beneficiaries, or very difficult assets (such as an active business or farm) can result in more compensation being requested and justified by the executor. In other situations, the appropriate fee will be less, for example, if the estate was large but its assets are mostly in a liquidated form (cash and a stock portfolio).

To assist with the subjectivity of this topic, over time the courts have developed a more objective guideline for executor compensation: up to five percent of the value of the estate. But it is important to keep in mind that when a will is silent on the compensation, the requested fee (and its approval) really is subject to the factors set out above, such as the work actually done by the executor.

2. specifically exclude compensation

We stated above that every executor is entitled to claim a fee, but when you are preparing your will, you can eliminate that possibility by stating explicitly in your will that the executor shall not receive compensation for carrying out this role. Estate lawyers usually recommend against this approach because really none of us know what will be involved in our estate administration and ruling out the possibility of compensation seems a little heavy-handed. Yes, your favourite niece may in usual circumstances carry out the work without a fee, but if litigation arises and the estate administration drags on for years, it may be that even your loving niece would think that the time and energy devoted to the estate is worth something.

If you decide to specifically exclude the possibility of your executor getting paid, you'd be wise to mention that when you are asking your executor to agree to being named to act in your will. On reading the will at your death and learning that there is no possibility of a fee, it may be that your chosen executor says Ciao to the job before starting it, if he or she feels that a fee is required. (As we discuss more in Mistake #40, even if the executor you ask agrees to be named in your will, he or she can still renounce, or decline, the job once the death has occurred. In other words, just because someone has agreed to be named, he or she may step aside when the work actually needs to be done.)

3. specifically provide for compensation

If you appoint a trust company to be your executor, the planning process will include a review of the fee agreement, which is attached to the will. This brings the issue of compensation right out in the open. Usually a trust company will not charge any fees for the planning work done with the clients and their lawyers; rather their fee will be collected only after the estate is administered. Depending on the age and health of the client, a number of years often pass between the planning of the will and the client's death and estate administration. During this time, a client will often be contacted by the trust company every few years to see if any significant changes have taken place requiring a will update. At that time you will have another opportunity to review and consider the fee agreement.

The fees charged by the trust companies in Canada are all very similar, with approximately 4.5 percent being charged on the first $500,000 of estate value, and then on a declining sliding scale on the additional estate value.

The clarity about the executor's fee when a trust company is appointed can be achieved even if you appoint an individual person. One estate lawyer advised us that people doing will planning usually don't put a lot of time or energy into the compensation issue, stating something like, "She won't take compensation, and if she wants to, let her sort it out with the beneficiaries."

A better approach may be to take control of the issue, build it into the will by providing a formula for calculating the fee, or stipulating an hourly rate or a flat fee.

You will also want to think about the timing of the fee. The law prevents an executor from "pre-taking" a fee, meaning paying him or herself before the estate administration is completed, but if you want your executor to have a partial fee as the work is done, this can be stated in the will.

4. leave a gift to the executor or provide for professional fees to be billed

An important point to keep in mind is that *executor compensation is taxable.* If your executor is a trust company, it will of course include its fees in its income, but you will want to think about the taxation issue for an individual named as your executor and ideally discuss it with him or her. It may be satisfactory to that person to have his or her compensation clearly set out, even though it will then be reported as income in his or her tax return. On the other hand, if the named executor is your adult child or niece or nephew, you may decide instead to give them a gift in your will or a larger share of the estate than they would have otherwise received.

Ironically some people, having made this decision, then go on to word such a clause with the preamble, "In lieu of compensation, I leave my executor a gift of $10,000." Well, uh, don't say that. The taxation authorities will very likely read such a provision as paying, yes, compensation.

If your named executor is a professional advisor, such as your accountant, whom you are naming primarily because of his or her business acumen and knowledge of your affairs, consider providing in the will that he or she can charge the estate for the work on an hourly rate, according to his or her regular rate.

recourse for beneficiaries

At this point, you might be wondering where the estate and its beneficiaries are left with all of this. What if the will doesn't mention a fee but then, as we have explained, the executor charges a fee and it is exorbitant? Or what if the amount is nicely set out in the will but the executor does a poor job, dragging the estate along for years as a little pet project?

The beneficiaries' opportunity to complain about the fee claimed by the executor arises when the estate is completed and they are requested by the executor to sign the release. At this stage, disgruntled beneficiaries can request what is called a *passing of accounts*, a court process during which the executor sets out the accounts, meaning what was done, how long everything took and the results achieved.

points to take away

▶ Executors of an estate are entitled to a fee and the time when you are planning your will and appointing one or more executors is a good time to think about their compensation.

▶ Appointing a trust company typically means that your will clearly states the fee methodology or attaches a compensation agreement binding your estate. Your opportunity to ask questions about the fees and how they will be assessed is during the estate-planning process or a follow-up will review. Don't hesitate to raise any questions or concerns you have at those times.

▶ If your executors are your friends or family, it is still important to at
least think about the work they will be doing and whether to specify
the payment of either compensation (referred to as such) or a gift. A
gift will not be taxable whereas a fee or compensation will need to be
reported as such by the executor.

PART 4

mistakes in estate administration

I CAN'T EVEN READ THIS THING!

MISTAKE #40

Overlooking opportunities to retain help with administering an estate

YOU ARE OUT FOR YOUR EARLY MORNING Sunday run through Stanley Park, and it's a perfect spring day. You're enjoying the time to think about your company's offsite strategy meeting, which starts tomorrow morning. When your cell phone rings, you see your spouse's name and you answer, ready for her caramel macchiato order, which you will fill on your way home. But instead she tells you your father has died.

Later, that phone call will be the clearest memory of your dad's death and the day he died suddenly in Toronto while he too was out for his morning jog. After the brief call with your spouse in which you heard the news, the rest of the day was a blur of travelling from Vancouver to Toronto, hugging your mom, starting to talk about the funeral, then taking the next steps. The offsite meeting was cancelled, your business partner graciously telling you to "take all the time you need." As Joan Didion says in *The Year of Magical Thinking*, the best-selling book she wrote after her husband's unexpected death, "Life changes in the instant."

And in that instant, or the days that follow, you can make one of the biggest mistakes in estate administration: missing the chance to hire professional help. In the middle of a loss like this—be it the death of your spouse, your parent, your sibling or your best friend—when you remember that you are named as his or her executor[1] and you feel overwhelmed by the prospect, keep in mind that you do have options. Because even as your colleagues, close friends and fellow volunteers in your charitable work are all encouraging you to step away from your responsibilities, you know that life goes on and some or all of the other aspects of your life will need to be picked back up in a couple of weeks.

So what can an executor in this situation do? You can:

1. Renounce your appointment as executor.

2. Remain on as executor but appoint a trust company to act as your agent in carrying out the estate administration but subject to you making all of the decisions that the company's representatives present to you.

3. Remain on as executor and do the work yourself, retaining assistance as needed, for example, a lawyer, accountant, real estate agent, valuator, a service to clean and organize the deceased's home and get it ready for sale and so on.

1. renunciation

There are several reasons why you may decide to not take on the job at all. Perhaps you didn't even know that you were appointed and if the deceased had asked you, you would have declined. Or perhaps you did agree when asked, but you weren't aware of the scope of the job, or something has changed in your own life, making this responsibility too much for you to take on now.

Another possibility is that the deceased person named an entire class of people to act—most likely all of the children—and after some discussion,

---

1 The terminology used to describe the person named in a will to administer the estate varies across Canada. For example, *estate trustee* is used in Ontario. For simplicity in the book, we use the term *executor*. As well, the phrases *executor and trustee* and *executor* are used interchangeably: the role of an executor is to carry out the administration of the estate and the role of the trustee in the estate of a deceased person is to administer any trusts set up from the estate assets. Usually these two roles are carried out by the same person, although in a small number of estates, the trustee and the executor may be different persons.

as a group you decide that the work can be done most effectively by only one of you acting . . . so the rest of you will renounce.

Whatever the reason is, be assured that sometimes the very best thing you can do for an estate is to not take on the job. Although you may feel that you are letting down a loved one, the job done by an executor who is too busy or overwhelmed for the task may result in a far worse outcome for the estate than if that executor had renounced, stepping aside at the time of the death.

We've already mentioned that sometimes a renunciation simply reduces the number of executors to a manageable one or two, but what if a renunciation means that no one is left to act? If the executors named in a will have all either passed away or are unable to act, the will is still valid and provincial laws apply as to the ordering of who in the next of kin can take on the job. The list starts with the deceased's spouse and moves through children and siblings until the first available person agrees to take on the position.

If you are thinking about renouncing, do not take any actions in the estate such as collecting the assets or inquiring into estate affairs. These types of actions are called *intermeddling* and when an executor signs the necessary paperwork to renounce the role, he or she is required to declare that no intermeddling has occurred, to avoid any later suggestion that any untoward steps were taken by someone without authority.

2. appoint an agent

Under this option, you remain on as the executor, but rather than being both the chief operating officer and the chief executive officer of the estate, you are opting to be only the CEO. This means that the day-to-day work of the estate administration, from cleaning out the deceased's home to doing the tax returns to selling the home or any businesses owned by the deceased—whatever the particular estate entails—is overseen and handled by professional trust officers who have seen and done it all many times.

If you are considering appointing a trust company as your agent, your best bet will be to meet with a representative of the company as soon as possible after you are notified of the death. They will review with you the work that they do and the fees they will charge the estate, and you will quickly get a sense if you like and trust them and can work well together with them on the estate. The estimated fees will vary greatly from one estate to another; the factors we covered in Mistake #39 on executor's compensation also affect the fees charged by an *agent* for an executor, factors such as the size of the estate and its complexity.

In weighing this option, including the estimated fees that the trust professionals discussed with you, keep in mind these points:

- An executor is always allowed by law to retain assistance, even if the will does not specifically state this.

- An experienced company carrying out the work is less likely to forget an important step.

- The trust officers will work with the beneficiaries and be their main liaison as to what is going on with the estate and when, for example, they can expect to receive their bequests or share of the estate.

- If conflict arises among the beneficiaries, you will have experienced guidance in dealing with it.

- In the unlikely event that an error is made in the administration, the "deep pockets" of a corporate trustee will protect you from personal liability.

3. carry on but hire assistance as needed

This is the "CEO and COO" approach, where you decide to oversee and organize the entire estate administration yourself. Although it is a big job, getting and staying organized, seeking out good advice, communicating well with the beneficiaries and hiring excellent professionals along the way will ensure that you stay on track. In the rest of the book, we'll look in more detail at all of those responsibilities.

points to take away

▶ Even if you have agreed to be named in the will of your friend or relative as his or her executor, when the death occurs, it may be very challenging for you to accept the appointment.

▶ There are options that you can consider if the idea of acting as the executor feels daunting. These include (1) completely renouncing the appointment; (2) appointing a trust company to act as your agent to carry out the administration, subject to you being the ultimate decision maker; and (3) hiring professionals to assist you with each step of the work.

▶ The best decision for you will depend entirely on your personal situation. Consider such factors as: where you live, your organizational skills, your available time over the coming year, especially over the first six months after the date of the death, and how you feel about working with the beneficiaries in the leadership role of being the estate executor.

I'VE ALWAYS BEEN A DO-IT-YOURSELF KIND OF GAL

MISTAKE #41

Making mistakes in retaining or working with the professionals you hire to assist you with the estate administration

SARAH ONCE READ SOME ADVICE about how to benefit the most from the doctor-patient relationship and the next time she went to her annual checkup, she prepared by writing down her questions, rather than hoping she would remember everything on the spot. Although this sounds like common sense, it is easy to forget the benefits of maximizing our professional relationships. Executors often make mistakes in working with the professionals involved in an estate administration, but doing so is rarely, if ever, a black-and-white event. Usually, the "mistake" is missing the chance to have a really great working relationship that serves everyone well.

hiring an agent

In Mistake #40, we discussed the option of hiring a trust company to act as your agent in a wide-ranging way, updating you regularly and bringing decisions to you that need to be made. For example, once the trust company's professionals have cleaned out and prepared the deceased's house for sale, the actual process of reviewing and accepting an offer to buy is something that you will do together with them. But even here, they will give you their guidance and advice on the best offer and why.

Before making the decision to hire a trust company as your agent, meet the trust officer, as you will be working with this person, often by email or phone, for months or even a couple of years. That initial meeting should provide you with a sense of the corporate culture and the attention to client service. Even if the trust officer you meet in the first meeting moves on to a new position before the estate is completed, the successor trust officer will most likely have similar experience and expertise. Go to this introductory meeting well prepared so that the officer can give you as much information as possible about what will be involved in the estate. Take the will and all other documents that you have found at this point in the estate.

And here is a nugget of advice for working well with a trust company acting as your agent: *follow the trust officer's advice most of the time.* One of the reasons you've hired an experienced trust company is because its professionals know what to do in a variety of situations. One trust officer mentioned a situation in which the trust company was hired as agent for the executor. In this estate, the deceased's adult child was living in the deceased's house and the executor (the trust company's client) was resisting the trust company's suggestion to either sell the home or collect rent from the child. But the child living in the house was only *one* of the beneficiaries of the estate and after the death, the house is no longer "Dad's house," it is an asset of the estate. Over time, the other beneficiaries of the estate will begin to have valid concerns about it being in limbo. In preventing the trust company from acting, the executor was making a mistake. If the executor had followed this experienced advice, he would have been authorizing the trust company to take actions in the best interest of the estate and for the benefit of *all* of the estate's beneficiaries.

hiring other professionals

In Mistake #40, we discussed taking on the estate administration *without* appointing an agent, and if you decide to take this approach, the adage

"Hire well, and the rest falls into place" applies in spades. In this scenario, you are not only the ultimate decision maker, but you are in charge of making sure that every step gets done—and that it gets done in a timely way.

Some of the professionals you may be hiring include a:

- lawyer

- accountant

- real estate agent

- valuator

- cleaning service

- property manager/interim business manager

In each of these situations, resist hiring the first firm that is referred to you. It doesn't take long to have a conversation outlining what you need and to request an estimate of the fees, process involved and time required. If a firm resists giving you an estimate of the fees or it takes a long time to get an estimate, move on.

Similarly, don't take a fee estimate as gospel. A lawyer who advises you that getting a court order to appoint you as the executor (sometimes called *probate*) will cost $5,000 in legal fees simply is letting you know the fee that *his or her firm* will charge. Maybe it is an appropriate estimate, maybe it is high—you will never know unless you seek out at least two fee estimates for each professional that you need to hire.

The other important advice is to stay on top of the timeline for each of the professionals you are working with on the estate. Unless you are the sole beneficiary of the estate, managing the expectations of the beneficiaries will be one of your most important and time-consuming tasks, so you will want to know who is doing what and when it will be completed.

There are a number of terrific time management and organizational systems available; even if you usually keep everything "in your head," as the executor of an estate, consider investing in a timeline-focused system that you can refer to when speaking with either the estate's professional advisors or its beneficiaries.

points to take away

▶ As an executor, when working with the professionals and advisors to the estate, treat the relationship in a professional, organized way, and both you and the estate will reap the rewards.

▶ Before appointing a trust company as your agent, meet with the trust officer and learn as much as you can from him or her about what will be involved in this particular estate as well as gaining a sense as to whether you would work well together.

▶ Be clear with everyone about your expectations in regard to timing and share these timelines with the beneficiaries. Try to stay a step ahead of everyone else in your timeline management so that the advisors are not waiting on you to make crucial decisions and the beneficiaries are not left in the dark as to what is going on in the estate.

▶ Avoid making the mistake of hiring great professionals and then not taking their advice. They have seen more estates than you have and although you are the executor and the deceased chose you for a reason, if you've hired people that you trust, *follow their advice most of the time.*

I ALWAYS LIKED THAT
SUSIE THE BEST

MISTAKE #42

Failing to fully understand the fiduciary nature of the role of the executor

ATTENTION! THIS IS ONE of the most important mistakes in the book, so if you are reading this before bed and feeling sleepy, we suggest setting it aside for the bus ride tomorrow.

A common and yet troublesome mistake made by executors and trustees[1] is forgetting (or never knowing) the gravity of the role. An executor is a *fiduciary* role, which means that an executor is responsible for providing the estate and its beneficiaries with the highest standard of care as he or she carries out the job. *Prudent* isn't a word we use much anymore, but it often comes up in descriptions of fiduciaries like executors, conjuring up a sense of acting carefully and cautiously. On a very practical level,

---

1 The role of an executor is to carry out the administration of the estate; the role of the trustee in an estate of a deceased person is to administer any trusts set up from the estate assets. Usually these two roles are carried out by the same person, so throughout the book, we use the terms *executor* and *executor and trustee* interchangeably. However, keep in mind that in some estates there is actually no ongoing trustee role (i.e., when the estate is immediately distributed out to the beneficiaries after the estate is administered, rather than being placed into longer-term trusts). As well, in a small number of estates, the executor may be a different person than the trustee.

examples of actions you might take as a cautious, prudent executor might include (but are definitely not limited to):

- cancelling your vacation when you realize that you are appointed as an executor and the death has occurred, so that you can make sure everything is locked down and protected;

- finding a lawyer whom you trust early in the process so that you have a really good idea from the outset what you need to do and by when; and

- getting several bids from property management firms before hiring one of them to clean out the deceased's home and get it ready for sale . . . and so on. As an executor you must take a belt-and-suspenders approach to life even if in your normal, day-to-day life, you might be an easygoing, laid-back kind of person.

Acting in the best interests of the estate and its beneficiaries is often made even more complicated if the executor is also one of the beneficiaries. This situation results in a potential conflict of interest, and in any fiduciary situation, any kind of conflict of interest is carefully avoided. For example, a lawyer (which is also a fiduciary role) will avoid wherever possible acting for both parties to a transaction, and, if for whatever reason, a situation like that arises, the code of ethics for the legal profession requires that all the clients be advised of the conflict of interest and provide their informed consent to it.

However, it is not quite so simple in estate matters because often we *purposefully* ask people we know and love to be our executor(s), so of course (a) they may also be a beneficiary of our estate (conflict of interest right there); and (b) they may be related to some but not all of the other beneficiaries (another conflict of interest). Professionals at the trust companies in Canada assured us that at the start of an estate administration, the trust officers review with any co-executors (often relatives of the deceased) what the role is all about and how an executor must completely set aside his or her own personal interests to do the job. The task of being an executor in the midst of a conflict-of-interest situation is not easy, as illustrated by these quite common situations:

- Samantha and a trust company are co-executors and trustees of Samantha's late husband's estate. A spousal trust was set up for Samantha from the estate's assets under the terms of the will. Upon Samantha's death, the balance remaining in the trust will be divided equally among her late husband's children from his first marriage. The will contains directions as to how capital and income distributions are to be made from the spousal trust, but in working with the trust company on matters such as distributions to herself and the trust's investment strategy, she will be in a conflict of interest situation at all times: what benefits Samantha will reduce what is left for her stepchildren. *Samantha must never forget the conflict of interest she is in and she must work with the co-executor and trustee to ensure that the terms of her husband's will are carried out as honestly and conscientiously as possible, in the face of the conflict of interest.*

- Adam is the executor of his late business partner's estate. The majority of the estate's net worth is in the value of the business. Adam is in a conflict of interest between his role with the estate and his co-ownership of the business. As the executor, he will want to obtain as high a price as possible for the deceased's share in the business; as the former business partner of the deceased, he will personally benefit by minimizing the valuation of the deceased's share. *Adam has taken on a role for his late partner that requires him to put the interests of the estate and its beneficiaries first, even to his own detriment. Transparency and objectivity will be required as Adam goes about valuing the business.*

- Jill is the executor and trustee of her dad's estate. According to her dad's will, Jill received her share of the estate paid out to her in full once the estate administration was completed. However, Jill's brother, Brian, has a gambling addiction and so his share of the estate was left to him through a lifetime trust, with Jill as the trustee. Brian has no children and at his death, the balance of his trust will be distributed among Jill's children. The conflict of interest here is a reversal of the situation with Samantha and her stepchildren: whatever is not paid out to Brian during his lifetime indirectly benefits Jill because of the ultimate distributions to her children. *Jill's primary concern and motivation must be to carry out the terms of the will, balancing the needs and interests of the lifetime beneficiary, Brian, with the interests of Jill's children, who receive the balance remaining in the trust on Brian's death.*

You may be ready to run screaming out into the street after reading about how easily conflicts of interest arise for an executor, but there are several ways to minimize the difficulty of these situations and to minimize the chance that you as an executor will run into problems:

1. Get advice. If you are working with a trust company as your co-executor, the trust company will assist you in understanding what you need to do to carry out your fiduciary role. As well, the trust company's very presence as a co-executor will probably make the situation more comfortable both for you and the beneficiaries. Appointments of a trust company as a co-executor are often made, at least in part, for the express purpose of adding an objective presence and influence.

2. Read and understand the will. This might sound obvious but the drafting of trust clauses can be very detailed and complicated and yet, if well understood, the clauses can provide you with a clear road map as to when distributions are to be made and for what purpose. If you don't understand anything in the will, ask the estate lawyer to go through it with you in plain English.

3. Be open and transparent about the conflict of interest and the issues that arise. In all aspects of life and relationships, it always feels so much more respectful when someone brings a difficult issue to us before he or she does anything about it that affects us. Rather than acting in an imperious manner because you are the executor, let the people affected by any conflict of interest situation know that you are well aware of it. Reassure them that you will do your utmost to act fairly and reasonably and only in the best interests of the estate, seeking advice and second opinions along the way. In other words, do your best to avoid a confrontation; estate litigation has a way of burning through the estate's assets rapidly and to no good end.

In summary, being an executor and a trustee is a unique role that requires a lot of skill and "emotional intelligence" at an already difficult time. Mix into that the possibility of a conflict of interest and you have a big job on your hands. However, the law is clear that unavoidable mistakes do happen for which an executor cannot be held responsible. If you become aware of an issue, promptly retain experienced legal advice and act honestly in what you feel was the estate's best interest at the time. You will then be headed in the right direction for carrying out well your fiduciary role as the executor and trustee of your loved one's estate.

points to take away

▶ There is no more unique or challenging role than being a fiduciary, such as an executor and trustee in an estate.

▶ The role requires the executor and trustee to act in the best interest of the estate, even when he or she would personally benefit from a different decision.

▶ Ways to get around the problems of being in an inherent conflict of interest include being open with the estate lawyer about what you need to know and understand, and transparent with the beneficiaries about the decisions you are making and your decision-making process.

DO I NEED TO MISS MY GOLF GAME?

MISTAKE #43

Not taking control of the estate from the outset

IN THIS MISTAKE, we will tackle the reluctance of some executors to confidently assume the leadership role that defines being an executor. The romantic comedy *The Wedding Planner* opens with Jennifer Lopez as the planner, headset in place, running a wedding rehearsal and telling everyone, including the bride, what to do and when. From a purely get-the-work-done perspective, an executor carrying on like that would certainly avoid the slow, creaking start that hampers a lot of estate administrations.

You may be thinking: *Well, an estate administration is a far cry from planning a wedding!* And of course you are right: administering an estate is a sombre duty and often the executor is carrying out the estate administration while also mourning the death of someone he or she loved. In many cases, the executor is also one of the estate's beneficiaries, so, for example, people who were once just brothers now may have an executor-beneficiary relationship as well. But the truth is that from the moment an executor learns of the death, he or she should assume the mantle of responsibility for administering the deceased's estate. As long as the will that appears is believed to be the last will of the deceased, the power and authority of the named executor arise from that document and ideally the work should begin immediately. You might think this is an exaggeration and that surely a grieving spouse doesn't need to worry about executorship duties until well after the funeral is over. But attending to the funeral and burial *is part of* the executor's role, so a husband or wife making those arrangements is already acting as the executor.

If you are not the spouse—perhaps you are a business partner of the deceased or an adult child—the first thing you will do is confirm who is taking care of the immediate arrangements for the deceased's remains, the funeral and the burial. Although this will likely be the deceased's spouse, if there is no spouse, then as executor you are responsible for this job; you must either do it yourself or ensure that someone else has it under control.

Sometimes the will or documents stored with the will contain relevant directions about the funeral and burial, so it is important to check for those written statements, particularly if there seems to be any confusion about the deceased's wishes.

Once the funeral arrangements are made, other responsibilities need to be attended to as soon as possible. A simple way to make sure that you are on the right track with your responsibilities is to drop into a branch of your bank and ask for its executor's checklist. [1]

It may be helpful to think of your executor role as separate and apart from your relationship with the deceased and the estate's beneficiaries. Although taking that perspective may sound heartless, the best and most effective executors always remember that the estate is a separate entity from the deceased. One of the first and most urgent tasks for the executor is to manage the transition from a living person's financial affairs (including asset ownership) into a deceased's estate. This point can be illustrated with an example.

Joe's wife, Sally, predeceased him five years ago. When Joe recently died, he was living alone in the family home close to downtown Halifax.

---

[1] Throughout the book we have mentioned our conversations with trust officers from Canadian trust companies; it may be helpful to keep in mind that each of these companies is a wholly owned subsidiary of one of the major Canadian banks. Accordingly, the branches of your bank or the deceased's bank will likely have copies of the helpful trust- and estate-related publications of their trust company.

Joe's house is full of valuable antiques and family heirlooms. Other assets in Joe's name include bank accounts, a couple of investment portfolios and a car that was being driven in the year before Joe died by his beloved grandson, Mike. You are Joe's eldest child and co-executor of his estate along with your sister, Joan, who is also Mike's mother. There are three other children in your family, but only you and Joan live in Halifax.

At least one of your siblings has a great interest in the family heirlooms, and in recent years, one of them, Bill, had occasionally queried Joe about what Joe's will said about the heirlooms. Joe steadfastly refused to discuss his estate planning with his five children, other than to tell you and Joan that you were the executors and that the original will was stored in his lawyer's vault.

Some of the immediate steps that you and Joan will need to take regarding the assets include:

- changing the locks on the house so that only the two of you have access to the house and its contents

- checking the house insurance to make sure that coverage continues and, if it does not, obtaining new insurance

- installing an alarm in the house and possibly installing smoke detectors

- retrieving the car from Mike and storing it safely

- speaking with the bank to let them know Joe has died and ensuring that the accounts can be accessed to pay funeral expenses

- starting the paperwork to transfer the accounts into your two names as the executors of the estate

- arranging for mail to be forwarded to you or Joan

You'll note that this list of to-do items in our example of the early days of administering an estate has an air of change and transition. That is appropriate and intentional. With their father now dead, the two executors need to make sure that everything is safe, with a view to one day distributing the estate according to the will. To do so, the executors must secure and button down the assets: the grandson no longer has his grandpa's approval to drive his car and the brother shouldn't be able to roam through the antiques unsupervised.

All of this may sound harsh, but in the days immediately following a death, you face one of your biggest challenges as an executor—the task of quickly figuring out where the assets are and what the urgent issues of concern are and how to address them. Failing to do these things at the outset often creates a problem later. In our example, if the deceased's house burns down without insurance or if the antique cabinet finds its way by FedEx to their brother's home in California because "Dad said I was to take it when we talked last year," the executors will have a big job on their hands to return the estate to its original status.

We wish we had an easy answer to how to balance the immediate workload of an estate administration with the unique aspects of being an executor, such as grieving the deceased at the same time as taking on a big job. "It ain't easy," and once you've been an executor, you will know the meaning of the saying, "Life goes on." From the moment an executor learns of the death, the work begins.

points to take away

▶ You were probably asked by the deceased to be his or her executor in part because of your leadership ability, so step up to the plate right after the death and become informed on important first steps.

▶ The sooner you can figure out what needs to be safely secured, the better it will be in the long run. In the early days after the death (the first week), your main priorities will be to arrange the funeral and secure any assets, including personal property, that may be at risk. Make sure that the estate assets are secure not only from fire and other damage but also from random "disappearances" that will be hard to unravel later.

▶ Although it may feel awkward at first, as the executor, you must be unbiased among all of the estate beneficiaries. While there is no need to be officious or domineering in your approach, try to keep the estate and its assets separate in your mind from memories of the life and times of the deceased. By taking this approach, you will have the greatest chance of effectively and appropriately carrying out your responsibilities.

WHAT, YOU WANT MY PHONE NUMBER TOO?

MISTAKE #44

Not communicating effectively with the beneficiaries of the estate

THERE'S A LOT TO DO AS AN EXECUTOR. If you drop into your bank branch to request an executor's checklist, it may list hundreds (okay, dozens) of tasks you need to get done. But sometimes how a task gets done is as important as just getting it checked off the list. This mistake is about being an *effective* executor, not merely an *efficient* one, by: (1) *communicating early* and often with the estate's beneficiaries; and (2) *managing expectations* of the beneficiaries appropriately.

If you have ever had a customer service role, you will know that the best way to work with customers, patrons or clients is to let them know upfront how long everything will take (worst-case scenario) and advise them about delays and snags before they become anxious wondering what's happening. In your executor role, think about this type of open communication as you work your way through the administration of the estate. Not only is this approach respectful, it also makes the process easier on you over the long haul.

communicating early and often with the beneficiaries

One of the lawyers we interviewed mentioned that she really wanted to tell us her pet peeve about estate administration. Curious, we said, "Sure, what's your pet peeve?" thinking it would be something like forgetting to file tax returns and having the estate owe a million dollars in interest and penalties. But no, it turns out that what irritated the lawyer was that people expected to attend an event, grandly called The Reading of the Will, at which the lawyer would crack open the sealed envelope (and maybe a nice bottle of port?) and read out the contents of the late person's will to the assembled family.

The actual reading of a will is far less dramatic, occurring, for example, as the executor stands in the cramped safety deposit box area of the bank, wedged between a desk and some storage boxes. Wherever the reading of the will occurs, one of the first things that the executor should do after he or she has reviewed the will is let the beneficiaries know what it says, to whatever extent is appropriate given the beneficiary's particular inheritance in the will.

For example, if a beneficiary is entitled to a *residual share* of the estate, meaning a portion of what is left after all debts and taxes are paid, then it is appropriate that he or she receive a copy of the whole will. If the beneficiary is simply receiving a sum of money or a teapot, then it is sufficient for the executor to give him or her a copy of the clause describing the gift.

With this suggestion, we are not referring to the letter-of-the-law requirements about a beneficiary's entitlement to a copy of the will or a clause of the will. The precise disclosure requirements and how they must be met (for example, by registered mail or personal service or whatever) vary by province. Instead, what we are recommending here is the executor adopting a non-legalistic approach, viewing the sharing of information as part of an overall open communication style as much for the long-term benefit of the executor as it is for the beneficiaries.

In other words, even though you may only be compelled by law to share the will with the beneficiaries when the application is made to the court for an order stating that the will is valid (often called *getting probate*), consider a different stance. If you were a beneficiary, would you rather have more information or less information, and would you prefer to have it sooner or later? Of course you would prefer more information, early on, and the executor who adopts a transparent, communicative style early in the administration will reduce or eliminate the possibility of conflict in the estate. Trust us on this.

managing beneficiaries' expectations

Trust officers who work for trust companies administer hundreds of estates over their careers and they emphasized to us that the administration of an estate usually takes a lot longer to complete than people expect. They recommend that executors "under-promise and over-deliver" when it comes to setting expectations in the minds of the beneficiaries as to how long it will all take.

Estate work involves many third parties: every company, creditor, bank, governmental department, employer, partner, store or magazine involved with the deceased person at the time of his or her death needs to be contacted, and then that third party will no doubt need to do something to move the estate along. Applying to the court for probate, filing taxes and waiting for the clearance certificate, cleaning and selling the house, selling the business, consolidating the financial assets . . . each task usually requires a much longer waiting period than you might expect.

This means that part of your communication with the beneficiaries has to be about how long it will be until they will receive their bequest or gift under the will, or their share of the estate. The answer to that question is, "it depends." A simple estate may wrap up in a year, the time period in which it is generally considered appropriate to administer an estate without some extenuating circumstances. However, keep in mind that the filing of the deceased's outstanding tax returns (if any), his or her terminal tax return, and the estate's final return can easily stretch out the time required past 12 months, as can delays caused by the requirements made by the third parties we mentioned above.

An estate in which there are disputes over the will's validity or any of its provisions, or an estate holding complicated or unusual property, will definitely take longer than a year to administer. In these situations, you will be working with an estate lawyer who will be able to provide you with the best (most conservative) estimates as to timing to share with the beneficiaries.

it's not "us versus them"

An executor is wise to avoid viewing the estate beneficiaries in an "us versus them" way. Clearly the executor has an important role to play in the deceased's estate, but the beneficiaries are also important parties, and as the estate administration nears completion, the executor will be requesting the beneficiaries to sign a release, releasing him or her from liability as the executor.

As we said earlier in this mistake, good customer service professionals let people know what's happening. As an executor, if you know there is some type of challenge or delay coming up in the estate, you and the estate lawyer should discuss communication with the beneficiaries and decide when it is appropriate to share information about the situation with them. Keep the beneficiaries well informed to the extent that you can. Long silences create suspicion, often resulting in the need to deal with hostility that has arisen simply because the beneficiaries didn't know what was going on.

points to take away

▶ There are lengthy task lists of the duties of an executor but two of the most important—and sometimes unstated—jobs are to communicate effectively with the beneficiaries and to be very clear with them about the length of time that it will take to administer the estate.

▶ After reviewing the estate timeline with your lawyer, take the opportunity to convey information to the beneficiaries well before they begin to have questions about what is happening, what they will receive under the will and how long the whole process will take. Even if *you* know why the administration is going slowly (for example, due to an insurance claim delay), the beneficiaries will not know this unless you tell them.

▶ An open and honest approach towards the beneficiaries of the estate will often save an executor time and possibly money, if conflicts are avoided, in the long run.

LET'S JUST TIDY THIS UP TODAY

 **MISTAKE #45**

Failing to get properly informed and organized and underestimating the work involved

WE'VE ALREADY DISCUSSED the early, urgent days of administering an estate when an executor needs to secure the deceased's assets, such as his or her home and all of the personal effects in it. And we have touched on the importance of communication with the beneficiaries to avoid the possibility of misunderstandings in the months ahead. But now we need to talk about the importance of getting really, really organized as you begin the work in earnest of being an estate executor. If you are a technology-oriented person, being organized will involve an electronic project management system; if you are more of a file folder and coloured pens type of person, get yourself to Staples and stock up on the supplies that you need.

When you look ahead to all that you have to do, you may feel over-whelmed and no wonder—administering an estate is a huge job and one way of looking at it may be to break it down into its components. By way of analogy, Julia Child's Boeuf Bourguignon recipe is a daunting novella to read, but if you look at its three steps (preparing the meat for the oven; letting it cook away for several hours; and adding the finishing touches) the whole thing makes sense and seems easier.

In an estate, the numerous tasks fall under five stages: getting organized; consolidating the estate; preparing the estate for distribution; distributing the estate; and winding it up. This mistake covers the first two all-important stages of organization and consolidation.

1. get organized

Getting thoroughly organized early in the estate administration will greatly simplify the work later and reduce the chance of missing something that the deceased either owned or owed.

Now is when you need to go through the deceased's document cases, folders, filing cabinets and computer files (hopefully you will have the password) to obtain birth and marriage certificates, property titles or deeds, mortgage documents, insurance policies, leases, tax records and last statements of credit cards. Look for evidence of financial assets, such as the last statements of bank and investment accounts and any actual share certificates, bonds, debentures and so on. If there is a key that looks like it belongs to a safety deposit box, try to locate the bank branch where the deceased did most of his or her everyday banking to see if the box is there.

Once you have assembled everything you can find, start to put together a listing of the estate assets and liabilities, based on your initial review of the bank and investment statements and other assets you know about. Now is also the time to carefully review the contents of the will together with other agreements that may affect the estate, such as a marriage contract or a separation agreement.

If you are unsure at all about whether the will adequately provides for the deceased's dependants, such as a common-law spouse or a former spouse, be sure to consult your estate lawyer as soon as possible. There may be notifications that need to be provided to alert people to his or her possible claim against the estate.

2. consolidate

Now is when you will be notifying organizations that the person has died and "turning off" the connections that formed part of his or her possibly active life. If you are the executor of an estate where the deceased person died an unexpected and early death, the period of notification and disconnecting will be onerous. On the other hand, this stage in an elderly person's estate may be straightforward by comparison.

Every executor quickly finds that you will need to prove your authority to do things on behalf of a now-deceased person. As you prepare to notify organizations about the death, arm yourself with at least twelve original funeral home death certificates, and also order (online if that suits you) the death certificate from the government registry in the deceased's province. Once you have that provincial death certificate, ask your estate lawyer to make you a half-dozen notarized copies of the death certificate, along with the same number of notarized copies of the will.

Use the documents you found in the organizational stage to make a list of who you need to call or write, and beside each organization note any relevant numbers (client identification numbers, account numbers, social insurance numbers, library card numbers). This type of information, along with proof of death, will be the first thing you need to produce when you call, write or attend at the office.

If you are aware that the deceased had email or social networking accounts, you will want to preserve the deceased's dignity by closing all such accounts and wrapping up blogs. Accounts to consider include all email accounts, of course, but also Facebook, LinkedIn and Twitter, and those are only a few of the possibilities. The deceased may have left usernames and passwords that are still in effect, but more likely you will need to contact each of the websites managing the social networking accounts used by the deceased. These websites will assist you in understanding the required steps to wind up the deceased's cyber presence appropriately.

Also at the consolidation stage—the notifying and gathering phase—apply for entitlements such as life insurance, the Canada Pension Plan death benefit, and any employment-related benefits, such as salary, vacation pay, stock options, and retiree or death benefits. You will need to open an estate account into which, over time, you will transfer all of the deceased's assets or the proceeds from their sale. This will also be the account from which you ultimately distribute the beneficiaries' shares of the estate.

The organization and administration stages of an estate are really important. More than just being the time when you set up a separate folder on your computer called "Estate," this is the time when you need to learn everything you possibly can about the deceased's affairs. Equally important, the consolidation stage marks the transition between the deceased's life as a human being, with all the connections and relationships that a life includes, and the administration of an estate.

points to take away

▶ In an estate, there are basically five steps: getting organized; consolidating the estate; preparing the estate for distribution; distributing the estate; and winding it up.

▶ Getting organized means finding out everything you can about the deceased's affairs in order to do a thorough job as the executor. Don't leave any stones unturned.

▶ Work methodically through the process and keep the beneficiaries informed as you get organized and consolidate the deceased person's affairs, the first two stages of the estate administration. Let them know that you are taking every possible step to make sure that you don't miss any of the deceased's assets or liabilities.

ENOUGH ALREADY!

MISTAKE #46

Failing to keep the estate administration moving ahead in a timely manner

BEING AN EXECUTOR MEANS hanging in there for the long haul, and some estates will require you to be patient and persistent over many months. It's a mistake to let an estate drag along slowly, a mistake that at the very least will result in the beneficiaries getting anxious and calling or emailing you frequently.

As we recommended for the early stages of an estate, once you are in the midst of the administration it is wise to have a plan of attack for everything that needs to be done. For clarity of thought, you may want to think of the work you need to do as three separate tasks: preparing to distribute, distributing and winding up.

1. preparing the estate for distribution

Now is when the executor works with the assets and liabilities to get the estate into a state where it can be distributed. It is here that you will be speaking with your lawyer about whether it is necessary to apply to the court for formal validation of the will in order to take these steps.

The shorthand term of *getting probate* may be familiar to you as the name for the court-validation process; the actual terminology varies among the provinces, however. In Ontario, for example, it is referred to as applying for and obtaining a certificate of appointment of estate trustee.

Whatever term is used in the deceased's province, the probate process is required whenever third parties advise the estate that they cannot transfer the deceased's assets without that court order. The reason third parties may take this position is because of the possibility of another will or because there are claimants to the estate that are not included in the will appropriately. Accordingly, a bank, for example, will not transfer a large account into an estate account unless its own compliance policy is met, and that policy may require the probate process. Speak to each financial services company where the deceased held accounts to determine its respective policies. The transfer of real estate always requires a probated will unless the real estate was held in joint tenancy.[1]

During this stage of an estate, you will also be:

- making sure that all of the deceased's debts are paid (likely the estate lawyer will assist you in this by publishing on behalf of the estate an announcement called a "notice to creditors" in the local newspaper);

- bringing the tax returns up to date and preparing and filing the T1 return and clearance certificate by no later than April 30th of the year following the year of death or six months from the date of death; and

- reviewing the investments for their appropriateness and perhaps selling them if the estate, for example, needs cash to make an interim distribution to the estate beneficiaries.

2. distribute

The stages of an estate do not necessarily all run sequentially. For example, you may decide to carry out the distribution of the personal effects in the

---

1 The death of a joint tenant means that the surviving joint tenant takes the interest over immediately upon death by the right of survivorship, without the requirement of a probated will. However, that general statement is subject to our comments in Mistakes #8 and #9 about assets held together by a parent and an adult child. In that situation, even if the jointly held asset is real estate, there should be evidence beyond merely owning it in joint tenancy indicating the parent intended that the child receive the asset as a gift after the parent's death.

first few months after the death. On the other hand, the distribution of the liquidated value of the estate (often called the *residue* of the estate, which is, practically speaking, the cash that accumulates in the estate account as the assets are sold) will take longer as you work your way through the taxes and the payments of liabilities.

However, one of the good-faith steps that you can take with the beneficiaries is to pay an interim distribution once you have paid all of the estate's debts and you have a very clear idea of how much will be required for taxes. Accordingly, at the time of filing the final tax return and requesting Canada Revenue Agency to issue a clearance certificate, discuss with the estate lawyer how much you can confidently pay out to the beneficiaries at this stage.

3. wind up

Once you have received the clearance certificate, the estate is ready to make the final distributions to the beneficiaries, either paid outright to them or into trusts set up in accordance with the will's terms. At this point, you will provide the beneficiaries with a final summary of the estate's assets, liabilities, expenses, interim distributions made, any compensation you are proposing to take, and the proposed remaining distributions, as well as a release, releasing you from your role as the executor. On receiving back all of the releases, you are ready to pay the final distributions and close the estate's bank account.

summary

The distribution and winding-up of an estate can be overwhelming and a cookie-cutter approach or adherence to a task list may simply not cover everything in each estate. The reason for this is also why trust officers really enjoy their work: every person's life is unique, so every estate is unique. Stay sharp throughout the estate administration and on guard for unique aspects of the deceased's life, will or estate that may be a little different than all the checklists. If you are concerned about something, review it with your estate lawyer. It is better to be on the cautious side whenever you are acting in a fiduciary role.

points to take away

▶ In the preparing-for-distribution and distribution/wind up stages of an estate you will likely be working closely with the estate lawyer to obtain probate and work towards readying the estate for distribution.

▶ Ensure taxes and all of the estate liabilities are paid or accounted for (with a sufficient amount held back for outstanding taxes) before making an interim distribution.

▶ Keep the beneficiaries informed. If they don't hear from you, they may assume the worst and think that you are either doing nothing or that there are big problems.

▶ Don't procrastinate or delay. There is a lot to do when administering an estate and leaving the work unattended will raise the ire of the beneficiaries, making your work more difficult than it needs to be.

I NEVER KNEW APIARIES
WERE SO COMPLICATED

MISTAKE #47

Incorrectly dealing with the estate assets (excluding the personal effects)

IF EACH OF US IS AS UNIQUE AS A SNOWFLAKE, as our Grade Two teacher liked to tell us, then each estate is also going to be unique. You may be lucky as an executor and discover that all of the estate assets were in a near-cash form when the deceased passed away, or maybe you will face greater challenges. This mistake considers assets in an estate on the far right side of the spectrum, the type that require you to be sharp as a tack.

The title of this mistake mentions apiaries—what do you know about running a beekeeping operation? If it is as much as we know, it's not a lot. Other types of estate assets that we heard about from trust officers included farms of all types (horse and dairy farms, as well as bee farms), partnership interests, manufacturing companies, sole proprietorships or sole professional practices.

If those all sound really interesting, keep in mind that the stories involved horses' lives that were at risk between the date of the farmer's death and the time someone else took charge; confidential patient files and drugs that needed to be accessed and then secured; and a payday that came on Thursday when the sole proprietor of an independent grocery store died on Wednesday. In other words, being an executor means stepping up, figuring out what needs to be done *now* and doing it.

In one estate during Jean's work with a trust company, the deceased had owned a golf course that had been booked months earlier for a wedding. A liquor licence was required for the event and even though the golf course was now an asset of an estate being administered by a trust company, the powers-that-be in the government still required the licence. The next thing she knew, Jean and her colleague next door were signing up for a liquor licence. Apparently a good time was had by all at the big event.

Once any crises have passed, your highest and best purpose as the executor is likely not to take on a new career as a horse breeder or a wedding planner. Instead, your role is to quickly ensure that appropriate care and management is in place for ongoing businesses and any other estate assets such as yachts, pets, expensive vehicles, extremely valuable collections or priceless jewellery. To find the appropriate person or business that you need to help you with complicated assets, consider speaking with:

- The estate lawyer. With years of experience, he or she may have a Rolodex at hand of possible property managers and other professionals you need.

- Your banker. Even if you are not retaining a trust company to be your agent-for-executor for the estate, if you have a long-standing relationship with your bank, chances are that your account manager can put you in touch with the bank's wholly owned trust company's professionals. Like an experienced estate lawyer, these trust professionals may have several ideas about where you can get the assistance you need. For example, trust officers in western Canada will likely know farm managers who will come into a farm as a tenant for a period of time to run the estate during its administration.

- The business itself. Perhaps the estate's business or farm has a key person running it now who can guide you at least in the short term. Over the longer term, you can decide if this person has the experience to continue on to wind up the business or assist in its sale.

- The business management and valuations group at a chartered accounting firm. Often such groups can step into an estate situation and run a business while at the same time determining the value of the business, preparing it for sale and ultimately assisting with the sale, perhaps even helping to locate a buyer.

Once the business or property is being looked after, turn your mind to the ultimate disposition of the asset. The deceased's will may provide that someone is to receive the asset *in kind*, meaning your job will be to transfer it to that named beneficiary as all or part of his or her share of the estate. Alternatively, the will may not specifically mention the asset, meaning that it will be sold, perhaps to a beneficiary at fair market value, or to an outsider, and the proceeds distributed as part of the estate.

Regardless of the specific nature of the asset's transfer under the will, find experienced advisors to assist you with all of the issues: valuation, taxation, the effect of the will on the transfer, the impact of the asset on the overall estate distribution, and the disposition. Retaining experienced professionals is important because as the executor you are in a fiduciary role for the benefit of the estate and the beneficiaries. It is one thing to make uninformed decisions on the fly for your own affairs, but quite another thing to do that when you are a fiduciary and responsible to others.

Whenever relying on expert opinions, be open to getting more than one opinion if the situation warrants it. Think ahead to how you will explain your process and your resulting decisions to the beneficiaries. Many times it is far easier to explain a decision if the time and effort have been taken to gain more than one opinion on a complex matter.

You also need to keep emotions out of the process. As the authors of a book, we can discuss these issues in the abstract, but in the day-to-day reality of an estate administration, assets like a small business or family farm often come along with a lot of history and interpersonal relationships. Keep the temperature down among the beneficiaries and others in the deceased person's circle by methodically working through the process of securing the asset, informing the beneficiaries along the way, and retaining the best assistance and professional advice that you can find.

points to take away

▶ One of your first jobs as executor is to secure all of the assets of the deceased person. If the assets are of a complicated or perishable nature, immediate and thorough research is required to find the appropriate way of caring for and managing them.

▶ Find good subject matter experts on the handling, valuation and ultimate distribution of complicated estate assets. These experts, for example, may recommend terminating long-term employees or assist you in calculating and filing the appropriate tax.

▶ With years of relevant experience, such experts can provide a wide range of relevant assistance.

OKAY EVERYBODY, TAKE WHAT YOU LIKE AND DON'T FORGET THE CAT

MISTAKE #48

Not dealing with personal effects in an effective manner

OHHH, THE DREADED PERSONAL EFFECTS! Simply hearing the term[1] makes seasoned trust officers shudder, having seen emotions run high over items like broken tea cups and vacuum cleaners.

The will is the executor's road map, but when it comes to personal effects, the will can be terse, or even silent, about how to distribute them. There may be a reference to a memorandum that the deceased plans to prepare sometime between the date of the will and his or her death, but often no such memorandum can be found.

As well, articles mentioned in the will may be missing or if the articles are around, there may be people who say that some items did not actually belong to the deceased. For example, if Tom's will says that his personal

---

1 *Personal effects* is a term used to describe all articles of personal or household use or ornament and all automobiles and their accessories. In other words, personal effects refers to property that is not real estate or financial in nature, and usually includes items belonging to the deceased, ranging from diaries and books to valuable art, jewellery and collections.

effects go to his surviving spouse, Hilary, from his second marriage, and the balance of his estate to the children from the first marriage, there may be some quibbling over whether the grand piano from the children's youth belongs as part of Hilary's personal property or part of the residue.

In light of the anxiety and stress that are often caused by a deceased's personal effects, a wise executor will swiftly locate and secure the personal effects and then take a measured and methodical approach to their distribution. Sometimes there is a rush to clean out the home, sort everything out, get the house sold and move on. But this can be a time when the old adage "Haste makes waste" applies, and as the executor, your job is to bring reason and order to the estate whenever possible.

After you have changed the locks on the deceased's home, or otherwise taken steps to make sure that none of the personal property goes missing, take an inventory and review the will's terms about personal effects. If it refers to the possibility that the deceased might have written a memorandum sometime between the date of the will and his or her death, try to track that down, although there is always a good chance that such a document was never done.

After taking these steps and speaking informally with the beneficiaries, you will start to get an idea about how to proceed. Gifts that are spelled out in the will or a memorandum are the most straightforward, but it is rare that all of the personal property will be covered. Many wills provide that the personal effects—or the remaining items after the specific gifts are made—shall be distributed among a certain group of people "as they shall agree," with no method given for how that agreement will be reached.

We're sure there are a lot of families like one we know where the division of Mom and Dad's artwork and personal effects involved everyone saying, "No, you take it." "No, no, you take it, you have always loved this painting," and so on. But there are also plenty of situations in which tempers flare and the personal property becomes the lightning rod for years of fighting.

Trust officers and estate mediators shared with us a number of really helpful tips on working through the distribution of an estate's personal effects, which you may find useful to consider as you wade into this aspect of estate administration:

1. Think about storing the personal effects for a while—even for three or four months. It can be a very difficult and emotional time immediately after the death and the funeral, and people may not be in the best state of mind for this particular discussion. What's the hurry? As long as the items are safe and secure, storing the items gives everyone time to reflect on which of the deceased's cherished personal items really matter to them, and the cost will likely be money well spent.

2. Once you have decided on a date to divide up the property, think about having a neutral third party present for the process. The beneficiaries are likely related to one another and sometimes people behave better if there is an observer or assistant from outside the family circle. If you as the executor are not a member of the family, then perhaps your presence alone is all that is needed, but if, for example, you are both the executor and one of the children, consider this option if you have the sense that a fight is brewing. Choose a person who everyone agrees is impartial and fair.

3. Decide whether the division is going to be simply by the number of items each person receives or by value. If it is by value, then use an independent appraiser to ascertain the values ahead of time. In reality, challenges over who gets what of the personal effects are rarely due to the monetary value of the articles, but if in the estate you are working on there are a number of items that people believe to be valuable, have them appraised.

4. Think about excluding spouses or partners of the beneficiaries at the time of the distribution. This may sound harsh, but we've heard many stories about the negative influence on the dynamics of an estate from individuals who are not beneficiaries but rather married to beneficiaries. We won't even attempt to guess why this happens, but experience indicates that the beneficiaries work best on their own. On the other hand, this suggestion may make no sense in your particular situation if the spouses are the only people in the group who bring an element of reason! Observe the dynamics of the estate on the personal effects situation and make the best call.

5. Come up with a methodology for distributing the items and then stick with it, such as having the eldest sibling select an item first and then so on down to the youngest, and then back up to the eldest, or drawing names out of a hat and having one round of selections, then drawing names again.

6. Encourage people to agree that everyone needs to leave with at least one to three items that are really important to them, regardless of the process used. Perhaps you can all agree that after the selection process is over, everyone will participate in a bartering process à la Halloween candy: "I got a lot of sour chews and prefer chocolate peanut butter cups, so let's trade some." Don't get mad if people lose their cool; if the executor stays calm and rational, other people will be more likely to act the same way.

7. If all else fails, do what corporate executors do and set a deadline for agreement and have those items that are not agreed upon by that date sent to an auction house for public auction. The irony of this approach is that often none of the feuding beneficiaries show up at the auction. This is a last-resort method and usually the beneficiaries will reach an agreement before the hundred-year-old tea set is actually shipped off.

points to take away

▶ One of your first jobs as executor is to secure all of the assets of the deceased person, including the personal effects. There will be lots of time to distribute them but make sure they are secure: if they "disappear" before they can be dealt with according to the will, especially out of the deceased's province, it will be very difficult to get them back.

▶ There are a number of ways in which you as executor can help to remove the emotion from the distribution of the personal effects, for example, by storing the items while you sort out how to divide them up.

▶ Remember that as the executor you are charged with the job of making tough calls and you may not always be popular. However, if you scrupulously avoid any perception of favouritism—towards your own interests or anyone else's—and use a careful, well-thought-out approach, you can successfully work through the distribution of personal property.

I THOUGHT I KNEW HIM
BETTER THAN THAT . . .

MISTAKE #49

Expecting the estate to go smoothly all of the time and being unprepared for the unexpected

AS AN EXECUTOR, it's a mistake to be caught off guard and potentially slowed down if you come across one or two surprises about how the deceased managed his or her affairs. Everyone's human! The first time Jean went to a bar mitzvah, she was so impressed by the accolades about the young man. How could he be so close to achieving world peace and curing cancer at the age of 13? And then she attended her *second* bar mitzvah and realized that part of these wonderful occasions is to celebrate to the max the positive attributes, steering clear of anything even mildly critical. The light bulb went off: bat and bar mitzvah speeches are like eulogies, the difference being that the person in question is there to enjoy the tributes!

Just as most teenage kids aren't perfect at age 13, the person whose estate you are administering may also have done things he or she shouldn't have or left other important tasks undone. When you become aware of these issues during the estate administration, it is easy to waste time bemoaning the unexpected challenge rather than simply addressing it head-on.

During our meetings with professionals from the major Canadian trust companies, all of whom have "seen it all," they shared with us a number of possible surprise occurrences for a first-time executor, and we will go through several of these below. However, an overriding point to keep in mind in dealing with any unexpected problems is to remember that you are in a fiduciary role. As a fiduciary, you must always act in the best interests of the estate and all of its beneficiaries. From a *practical* perspective, acting in a good-faith, honest manner requires you to become well informed on whatever issues and options are in front of you before you take action or make a decision.

1. assets held unexpectedly in joint tenancy

Throughout our lives we tend to hold some or all of our assets jointly with our spouse or partner. The legal impact of this—*a joint right of survivorship*—is most times exactly what we want. At the time of the first partner's death, the clear intention is for the joint account or house to be transferrred as easily as possible to our surviving partner.

Holding assets jointly with people other than our spouse, usually later in life, can be a little murkier. The question then often asked is, what was the deceased's intention in doing this? At the death, the executor may not be sure whether the account, for example, is an estate asset or rightfully belongs to the surviving joint owner, perhaps an adult child of the deceased or a caregiver.

What the law says about this would easily fill a legal memorandum and even the Supreme Court of Canada has opined on the topic in recent years. The law hopes to find, in any situation of joint assets, evidence as to what the deceased *intended* to happen. If there isn't any evidence, then there is a *presumption* that a surviving spouse was intended to receive the jointly held asset account and a presumption that an adult child was *not* intended to do so.

However, as an executor, you do not want to guide the estate through litigation to get the final answer. A far better approach is to speak as soon as possible with the surviving joint owner to explore the fundamental question of whether the deceased intended for the joint asset to be a gift to the joint owner. Some questions for discussion include:

- What is the position (opinion) of the joint owner? Is the joint owner even taking the position that the asset belongs to him or her?
- If yes, then when did the asset become jointly held (or when was the account opened if it was always a joint bank account)?
- What was the purpose of the account?
- Who put money into the account (or the house) and who used it?
- What was the believed intention of the deceased and is there evidence of this?

Ideally you will be able to resolve the situation either on your own with the surviving joint owner or with the help of the estate lawyer. If it appears that the matter is becoming heated quickly, consider retaining a mediator to assist you and the person taking the position that the asset belongs to him or her. Often a mediator charges a flat rate for a day with disputing parties, and it is possible that the matter can be resolved in a day.

2. assets with outdated titles

One trust officer mentioned to us a simple matter but one that arises fairly often when the last surviving spouse passes away and still lives in the family home of 50 years. When Josie dies, leaving her husband Joe surviving her, often no one will bother to change the title to the house into only Joe's name. This means that at Joe's death ten years later, it is still registered in the names of Josie Romano and Joe Romano, as joint tenants. What sounds like a small detail becomes a big nuisance when a buyer for the house is anxious to close the purchase from the estate. Similarly, a title to an estate property may still have outdated mortgages on it that were paid off long ago.

The moral of these stories? Check the property title before you list it for sale in order to avoid surprises and delays in the process of trying to liquidate the estate.

3. loans or guarantees made by the deceased or payments being made to others

Professionals who work in the area of trust and estate planning and administration know that many people have a story of some sort that emerges during the administration of an estate. We are not just talking about titillating secrets; one of the most common surprises is a person of apparently very modest means who leaves charities millions of dollars.

In a similar vein, an executor may discover that the deceased had loaned money to people, guaranteed loans or provided mortgages, none of which is clearly referred to in the will or other documents. The sooner that these arrangements can be discovered the better, so as we recommended earlier, from the time you learn about the death, set the stage for open communication with the beneficiaries and others with whom the deceased was close, either through business dealings or in his or her personal life.

By establishing open lines of communication, you will be more likely to hear from people if the deceased guaranteed their small business, loaned them some money or gave them a mortgage on the house. While it is impossible for us to hazard a guess about the variety of situations you may face, keep in mind that you are not negotiating on behalf of the deceased but rather on behalf of the estate. Upon his or her death, the perspective of the deceased may not match what is in the best interest of the estate and its ability to carry out the terms of the will.

For example, if the estate will be funding several trusts for minor children, renegotiating a mortgage on the deceased's brother's home will be a different matter for the executor than it may have been for the deceased who was in the prime of his income-earning years when he granted the mortgage to his unemployed brother.

The right answers to any situation of an unexpected loan, guarantee or stream of payments is that "it depends" and by saying this we are emphasizing the fact that being an executor is a *discretionary* role that can't be done by rote. Whenever you are unsure how to appropriately exercise your discretion as an executor, seek and carefully consider the counsel of an experienced estate lawyer.

4. unfiled tax returns in Canada or other countries, especially the United States

If you are a dutiful Canadian and file your tax return each year, it may come as a surprise that a number of people are not as dutiful, and one of the first things you will need to do as an executor is to make sure that all past tax returns have been filed and the taxes paid. It's important to do this early in the administration because the catch-up process can take a while, and before you are able to do the final tax return and request a clearance certificate, all prior years will need to be filed and assessed.

A further wrinkle involves a citizen from another country who dies as a Canadian resident. Some countries, such as the United States, require their citizens to file tax returns each and every year in that country *even if they do not reside in the country of that citizenship.* So if you are an executor facing a situation of unfiled foreign tax returns, again, all we can say is don't be surprised (this happens more than you might think!) and get on it quickly.

points to take away

▶ None of us is perfect and that doesn't change just because we pass away. As an executor, expect the unexpected.

▶ Early communication with the beneficiaries and anyone else who may have an interest in the estate will assist you in finding out about potential challenges sooner rather than later.

▶ Finding a practical solution that is in the best interest of the estate and the beneficiaries' interests under the will is preferable to an expensive estate dispute. Through your own discussions with people involved and the assistance of an experienced estate lawyer or mediator, do what you can to resolve problems wisely and with minimal acrimony. Your goal is to wisely administer the estate, not have its activities reported in the *Canada Supreme Court Reports.*

BACK SEAT DRIVING
IS A SNAP!

MISTAKE #50
Being a belligerent beneficiary

IN WRITING ABOUT COMMON MISTAKES in estate administration up to this point in the book, we've probably been a bit like schoolmarms in our admonishments to executors: act quickly, communicate with the beneficiaries, expect the unexpected and file taxes! If you are an executor you are likely quite weary of it all by now, so here we are putting the shoe on the other foot and addressing the mistake of being a mean-spirited or overly impatient beneficiary.

starting off on the right foot

As a beneficiary, start off on a positive note with the executor. Make it clear that you appreciate the role he or she is taking on and that you will do whatever you can to assist. If the executor is someone you know well, perhaps a sibling or an uncle, try to set aside past history that isn't positive. Resolve to come to the end of the estate administration with your relationship at least as good as it was at the time of death. If there are tasks that you believe should be getting done, offer to help.

Clarifying expectations (yours, the other beneficiaries and the executor's) will help everyone. The law allows an executor about a year, generally speaking, from the date of death to administer the estate and transfer the assets to the beneficiaries. Although this sounds like a long time, the debts and taxes also need to be paid before the distributions can be made, so the year usually flies by. Meeting with the executor early in the 12-month period after the death to discuss his or her approximate timetable will take away those nagging questions about what is happening and why it is "taking so long."

Once you have agreed on an approximate timetable of events, such as receiving the will, applying to the court for probate and so on, promise the executor (and keep your promise!) that you won't be in touch with questions about what is going on. By showing this respect to the executor, you increase the likelihood of the executor letting you know when the house sale is being delayed for some reason or the court is taking longer to issue the probate document than expected.

Trust officers working for a trust company that has been appointed as an executor or co-executor do their very best to keep the lines of communication open with the beneficiaries of an estate. Privately they will tell you that sometimes beneficiaries don't listen very well to their explanations about delays. For example, the executor can send a transfer form to each bank that holds funds in the deceased's name—and then those companies can take weeks to respond. Later, the executor can file the application for probate, or whatever the term is in the applicable province—and then the court takes four months to issue the certificate. You get the picture. Agree with the executor on a reasonable schedule and then let the executor do his, her or their work.

Another tip is to consider speaking on your own behalf to the executor and not delegating this task to your spouse. We heard this tip several times from professional trust officers, who typically end up explaining everything twice when a beneficiary, for whatever reason, asks them to work with his or her spouse but then later wants clarification. Always remember that *you* are the beneficiary of the estate, not your husband or wife, so at the time the estate is wound up, *you* are going to be asked to sign a release approving its administration. By asking the executor to work with your spouse or anyone else, instead of you, you may be requiring the executor to explain things repetitively (especially if other beneficiaries make the same request), taking the executor away from doing other estate-related work.

when things go wrong . . .

So far everything we have suggested in this mistake assumes that the executor is well-intentioned, hard-working and wants to do a good job. Of course there are situations where a beneficiary will suspect early on that the estate will either be handled very slowly or not at all, or that it will be administered ineffectively and perhaps even dishonestly. If this happens, hire a lawyer experienced in estate matters who can review the will and the situation, as you understand it to be, and then advise you on the best approach. Just being alerted to the fact that you have retained counsel to represent you may be all that is required to motivate the executor to act. (On the other hand, the lawyer may tell you to cool your jets).

Our final tip to beneficiaries is to get advice on the best way to receive your inheritance, from both a tax perspective and that of family law. In most provinces, an inheritance is not included in the assets that are divided upon a separation as long as it has been kept separate from the marital assets. Even if your relationship is sound, act from an informed position. As one experienced estate planner put it, "It's great if beneficiaries use their inheritances to pay off the mortgage, but they should at least know what they are doing when they do that."

points to take away

▶ As a beneficiary, do your best to support and assist the executor and work towards establishing a reasonable timetable for the estate's key steps.

▶ On the other hand, seek experienced advice if your intuition tells you that the estate is being mishandled. An executor is in a fiduciary role and all of the dealings with the estate must be in the best interests of the estate and its beneficiaries, and must be handled honestly, ethically and in good faith. It may be impossible to return the estate to its original status if the executor is allowed to act inappropriately for a period of time.

▶ Seek legal (tax- and family-law-related) advice before you receive your inheritance.

GLOSSARY

ADMINISTRATOR OF AN ESTATE—the person appointed by the court to administer a deceased person's estate when there is no will. Intestacy legislation in each province sets out the priority list of who may apply to be appointed as the administrator of an intestate person's estate.

ADVANCE DIRECTIVE—a term sometimes used to describe the document setting out a person's wishes for health and personal care when he or she is no longer able to make those decisions independently. The precise terminology varies by province, as do the specific requirements to ensure the document is binding.

AGENT—commonly used to refer to a person authorized by another person to act on his or her behalf. In an estate-planning context, the term is usually associated with documents such as personal directives and advance directives, which can use the term or a form of the term, such as *health care agent*, to refer to the person authorized in the document to make personal and health-care-related decisions on behalf of the person preparing the directive. Each province has its own terminology in this area of the law.

ALTER EGO TRUST—often referred to in the same context as a joint partner trust, these trusts can be set up by Canadians over the age of 65 where the assets and circumstances of the individual or the couple indicate that establishing such a trust is warranted. Although a discussion with an experienced professional is required before proceeding to set up an alter ego or joint partner trust, it is generally suggested that these trusts are appropriate for individuals with substantial assets who wish to avoid or minimize probate fees or estate administration taxes, who prefer to keep their affairs after their death private, and who are willing to incur the costs of setting up and maintaining the trust.

ATTORNEY—in the United States (and its television shows!) this is the main term used to describe a lawyer; this usage causes confusion in Canada, where the term is most often used to describe the attorney appointed under a power of attorney to assume a fiduciary role under and according to the terms of the power of attorney. The person appointed in this way to be an attorney for another person does not need to be a lawyer and typically is a trusted family member or close friend.

BENEFICIARY—an *estate beneficiary* is a person who receives a share of a person's estate. The share can be a single item or money paid directly to him or her or into a trust for the person's benefit over a number of years, for example, until the beneficiary reaches a certain age. A residual beneficiary receives a stated share of the residue of the estate.

A *trust beneficiary* has an interest in a trust and the exact nature of that interest is described in the trust document, deed or agreement. If the trust is set up at the time of someone's death, then the trust beneficiary's specific interest will be described in the will.

BENEFICIARY DESIGNATION—refers to the declaration of the intended recipient of a financial asset upon the death of the asset's owner or named insured. Such assets include an insurance policy, a registered retirement savings plan (RRSP), registered retirement income fund (RRIF) and tax free savings accounts (TFSA.) Beneficiary designations can also be made or changed in the will. On the face of it, beneficiary designations can appear to be a simple way to benefit another person upon death, but it is essential to understand how beneficiary designations in the plans themselves (such as an insurance policy or RRSP) work together with one's will planning and/or the consequences of changing a beneficiary designation in the will.

As well, beneficiary designations are subject to provincial legislation, so it is essential to be advised on the requirements of a valid beneficiary designation in the province of residence before proceeding with such a designation.

BONDING—refers to the bond-posting process required in some estate situations, with the specifics of such requirements varying across Canada. A bond is posted to safeguard the estate, its beneficiaries and its creditors against the possibility of the improper administration of the estate and typically is required if: (1) none of the executors applying for probate or an appointment as estate trustee are Canadian residents; (2) the executors applying are not named in the will as executors (i.e., the will is valid but for some reason the named executors are unable or unwilling to act as executors); or (3) the deceased died intestate (without a will) such that an administrator needs to apply to administer the estate in accordance with the intestacy legislation. In these situations, the court requires the applying persons to post a bond to secure and safeguard the estate against possible wrongdoing by the executor(s) or administrator(s).

CERTIFICATE OF APPOINTMENT OF ESTATE TRUSTEE—a term used in at least one province to refer to the document historically called *probate* or *grant of probate*. It is the court's statement that this is indeed the last will of the deceased and that the executor named in it is authorized to carry out its terms.

CODICIL—a document that changes one or more specific parts of a will and confirms that the rest of the will remains valid and binding. A common use for a codicil is to substitute the will's named executor or named guardian with a different person or persons, due to changes in relationships or place of residence, and then to confirm that the rest of the will is still intact.

DEPENDENTS—the common usage of the term is to describe people who are financially reliant; however, from a strictly legal perspective the term *dependent* is determined by the context, and also the definitions of dependents vary from province to province. For example, in some provinces and in some situations, a cohabitant in a long-term relationship (sometimes colloquially referred to as a *common-law spouse*) may have legal status as a dependent in the same way as a married spouse. This area of the law is complex, however, and it is essential in estate planning to retain experienced legal counsel so that this professional can ensure you are aware of those dependents who may have a claim on your estate.

DESIGNATIONS—*see Beneficiary Designation*

END-OF-LIFE CARE—this term usually refers to the decisions that need to be made about the appropriate health care to be provided as an individual nears the end of life, such as pain management and available support procedures. These decisions are usually required when the individual is unable to make such decisions independently. If the individual has planned in advance, he or she will have appointed a substitute decision maker in a personal directive; failing that, provincial legislation guides the attending physicians about who to consult on these decisions.

EXECUTOR—the person named in a will to administer the estate. If the will appears to be valid, the power and authority of the executor to act begins immediately upon the death of the person who signed the will. Sometimes in order to transfer the deceased's assets according to the terms of the will, the executor must obtain a certificate of appointment of estate trustee (probate) from the court. In very occasional situations the validity of the will is contested. If this happens a court application will be required to determine the outcome.

EXECUTOR AND TRUSTEE—in almost all estates, the executor and trustee are the same person performing two roles: the executor administers the estate and distributes the deceased's assets according to the will, whereas the trustee administers any trusts set up for beneficiaries under the will's terms. In occasional cases, the role of trustee is carried out by a different individual than the executor, or, in some situations, a trust company will be asked to administer the trusts after the completion of the estate administration by a relative or a friend.

FIDUCIARY—a party entrusted with the responsibility to carry out the care and management of property, acting always in good faith and strictly for the benefit of another party. In an estate or trust situation, fiduciary roles include: an attorney under a power of attorney, an administrator of an intestate estate, an executor of an estate where there is a will, and any type of a trustee. Each of these roles requires the person or trust company to hold and manage assets for the benefit of another, according to the highest standard of care.

GUARDIAN—there are several uses of this term, including its use and definition in several different ways in provincial legislation. The most common usage of this term in will planning is to the guardian appointed to raise any minor children of a deceased person or couple. This appointment is always subject to the court's confirmation of the guardian's fitness for the responsibility. A guardian steps into the parenting role, excluding the financial management of the assets for the minors; the financial management function is carried out by the trustee named in the will. Another common use of the term *guardian* is in reference to a person appointed by the court to be the guardian of a person found by the court to be unable to make personal and health-care-related decisions.

GUARDIANSHIP—the process used to describe the appointment of a guardian or the relationship between the guardian and the person for whom the guardian is responsible.

HEIR—a term used interchangeably with but less frequently than *beneficiary*.

HOLOGRAPH WILL—a will written entirely in the handwriting of the person preparing the will. It is not valid in all provinces.

IN TRUST—a phrase that can create uncertainty because it is often used to describe an asset such as a bank account intended for the benefit of, for example, children, but upon examination, a complete set of trust terms and provisions is missing. To establish a trust for the benefit of someone else, a trust deed, agreement or document is required to ensure that all points are addressed, such as when the assets are to be distributed, at what age and for what purposes.

INCOMPETENCY—commonly used to refer to an absence of physical or mental abilities; however, in an estate-planning context it is important that the meaning be defined and the determining factors of incompetency be clearly specified. For example, if a power of attorney is to be effective only if and when mental incompetency occurs in the person who signed the power of attorney, the document needs to clearly state who will determine that incompetency has occurred, for example, two physicians or the person's attending physician.

INTESTATE—a person who dies without a valid will or who has a will that does not address all of the person's property. For example, if a will only distributes the person's personal property, he or she would die intestate with respect to all of the other property owned at death, such as real estate and financial assets.

INTESTACY/INTESTATE ESTATE—the situation that occurs when a person dies intestate (see above).

JOINT PARTNER TRUST—often referred to in the same context as an alter ego trust, these trusts can be set up by Canadians over the age of 65 where the assets and circumstances of the individual or the couple indicate that establishing such a trust is warranted. Although a discussion with an experienced professional is required before proceeding to set up an alter ego or joint partner trust, it is generally suggested that these trusts are appropriate for individuals with substantial assets who wish to avoid or minimize probate fees or estate administration taxes, who prefer to keep their affairs after their death private, and who are willing to incur the costs of setting up and maintaining the trust.

JOINT TENANCY—a form of ownership commonly associated with real estate and bank accounts. Each joint tenant has an undivided interest in the property. In an estate-planning context an important characteristic of joint tenancy is that if one of the joint owners dies, the property transfers to the surviving owner or owners through the right of survivorship and not through the deceased owner's will. This point is subject, however, to recent Canadian cases indicating that where a parent holds property in joint tenancy with an adult child, additional evidence may be required to establish that the parent intended to transfer the interest to the child.

LAST WILL AND TESTAMENT—a verbose term containing three too many words; a *will* is the appropriate term. Simply because a document is called *a last will and testament* does not preclude the possibility of the testator preparing and signing a later will that will then take precedence assuming that it is otherwise valid.

LIVING WILL—a colloquial term used more frequently in the past to describe the person's wishes about health and medical care, particularly at the end of life. Over the last 20 years, the provinces have enacted legislation specifying how best its residents can set out these wishes, and these documents have different names across the country, such as advance directives, personal directives and powers of attorney for personal care.

MENTAL INCAPACITY—commonly refers to an absence of the mental ability to make some or all of the personal and financial decisions that a person usually makes independently. However, in an estate-planning context it is important that the meaning be defined and the determining factors of mental incapacity or incompetency be clearly specified. For example, if a power of attorney is to be effective only if and when mental incapacity or incompetency occurs in the person who signed the power of attorney, the document needs to specify who will determine that such incapacity has occurred, for example, two physicians or the person's attending physician.

MINOR—a person under the age of majority in the province of his or her residence.

PERSONAL DIRECTIVE—a term sometimes used to describe the document setting out a person's wishes for health and personal care when he or she is no longer able to make those decisions independently. The precise terminology varies by province, as do the specific requirements to ensure the document is binding.

PERSONAL EFFECTS—articles of personal and household use or ornament and all vehicles and their accessories.

POWER OF ATTORNEY—a document in which a person (often referred to as the *donor*) appoints a person to be his or her attorney to hold and manage some or all of the assets according to the terms of the document. A power of attorney always terminates upon the death of the donor. A power of attorney is a flexible concept; for example, it can commence as soon as it is signed, continuing until the donor's death, or it can become effective only upon the occurrence of a specific event such as mental incompetency, continuing until death.

POWER OF ATTORNEY FOR PERSONAL CARE—this term is used in some provinces to refer to the document that appoints an individual to make personal-care and health-related decisions for the donor (person whose power of attorney for care it is) when the donor is no longer mentally competent to make these decisions independently.

POWER OF ATTORNEY FOR PROPERTY—a term used in those provinces that have the term *power of attorney for care* to distinguish the two types of powers of attorney. Powers of attorney for property deal only with financial and property matters, not decisions of a personal or health-related nature.

PROBATE—in some provinces, refers to the process carried out by an executor filing certain required documents with the court to obtain a grant of probate or letters probate, which is the court's statement that this is indeed the last will of the deceased and that the executor named in it is authorized to carry out its terms. Other provinces use different terminology, such as applying for a certificate of appointment of estate trustee.

PROBATE FEES OR TAXES—each province has its own fee schedule for the fees charged on the filing of an application for a grant of probate or certificate of appointment of estate trustee (the terms vary across Canada; in Ontario it is called the *estate administration tax*). The fees are based on the value of the estate assets. Most provincial governments have a website setting out the provincial probate fees.

PUBLIC GUARDIAN/PUBLIC TRUSTEE—the precise role, functions and names of these public offices vary across Canada; however, each province has a provincial governmental arm that is essentially responsible for protecting the interests of minor children and persons who are unable to make financial and personal decisions on their own and that is responsible for administering the estates of certain deceased persons when no one else is able to take on this role. These offices have limited resources, and particularly in the areas of assisting adults who require help with financial matters, personal and health care decision-making or estate administration, these public bodies will quite appropriately look to available family or close friends to assume these functions wherever reasonably possible.

RENUNCIATION—in an estate administration context, renunciation means formally declining to act as the executor named in a will, after the death of the person whose will it is. Renunciation must be done formally by signing the appropriate document to be included in the application for probate (or whatever the court filing process is called in the province of the deceased's residence). A named executor who intends to renounce must not take any actions in the estate (sometimes called *intermeddling*).

RESIDUE—in a deceased's estate, the residue is the value of the estate remaining after the payment of all debts and taxes and the distribution of all specific gifts (such as personal property or specific items or sums of money). Those beneficiaries who receive a share of the residue are referred to as *the residual beneficiaries.*

SETTLOR—the person transferring property to a trust, where it will be held by a trustee for the benefit of the beneficiaries, according to the terms of the trust agreement, deed or document.

SPOUSAL TRUST—in a will context, a spousal trust provision directs that some or all of the estate residue is to be placed in a trust for the surviving spouse and managed for the benefit of the surviving spouse, usually for his or her lifetime. The specific terms of the trust, such as how it is to be managed and used, and who will receive the balance in the trust at the surviving spouse's death, are set out in the will.

SUBSTITUTE DECISION MAKER—a term used throughout the book to refer to the named attorney or agent under a power of attorney or a personal directive or advance directive. Some provinces also use this term in their relevant legislation on personal directives and powers of attorney. It is important to clarify what exactly it means in any specific context: in some situations the substitute decision maker may be appointed to make personal and health care decisions; in others, the role may pertain to financial decision making and management.

TAX CLEARANCE CERTIFICATE—executors and administrators typically wait to receive the clearance certificate from the Canada Revenue Agency (CRA) before distributing some or all of the estate assets. A clearance certificate certifies that all amounts for which the deceased person was liable to CRA for the tax years up to the date of death have been paid. Distributing the estate without ensuring that there are sufficient assets left in the estate to pay CRA means that the executor or administrator assumes personal liability for the tax owing.

TENANTS IN COMMON—this form of ownership is best understood in comparison to joint tenancy (see above). In contrast to joint tenancy, owners as tenants in common have an interest in the property that transfers upon the owner's death according to the terms of the owner's will or intestacy legislation if there is no will.

TESTAMENTARY TRUST—refers to a trust set up in a will after the administration of the estate and the distribution of immediate gifts, such as personal effects and specific gifts of money or other assets. Trusts set up in a will are governed by the terms of the will, covering such items as the length of the trusts, how the assets are to be used and for whom, and who is to receive the remaining assets when the trusts are wound up.

TESTATOR—a person who prepares a will. *Testatrix* is an old-fashioned reference, meaning a female testator, but the term testator is now commonly considered gender neutral.

TRUST—often described as a three-part fiduciary relationship among a settlor, a trustee and the beneficiary. In setting up, or *settling*, a trust, the settlor transfers legal title to the trust property to the trustee and the beneficial interest to the beneficiary or beneficiaries, as described fully in the trust document (sometimes referred to as a trust deed or trust agreement). The beneficiaries may receive income or capital from the trust during their lifetimes or their interests may only be received when the lifetime beneficiary or beneficiaries pass away. Trusts are extremely flexible, depending on the settlor's intentions.

TRUST OFFICER—a professional employed by a trust company who is assigned to oversee and administer the trust company's appointment as a corporate executor, an attorney under a power of attorney, an agent for an individual acting as executor, or as the trustee of a trust. A trust officer's experience is often matched with his or her assigned estates and trusts so that the estate or trust benefits from the trust officer's past experience in working on that particular type of estate or trust.

TRUSTEE—a fiduciary charged with the responsibility of holding and administering assets in a trust for the sole benefit of the trust's beneficiaries, according to the highest standard of care. In an estate, the executor often is also the trustee of any trusts set up in the will.

WILL—a legal document setting out the testator's instructions about the disposition of his or her assets after death. A will also names an executor to carry out the administration of the estate and the distribution of the assets in accordance with the will; a guardian for the testator's minor children, if any; and a trustee to hold and manage any trusts funded by estate assets. Often the executor and trustee are the same person. A well-drafted will requires competent experienced advice from someone who is knowledgeable about the particular legal requirements of a valid will in that province as well as the components of an effective and unambiguous will.

INDEX

mental incompetency, xiv, 243, 246
  defined, 245
  tests for capacity, 71–72
minor children
  assets in name of, 135–36
  defined, 245
  guardianship of, 55, 56–57, 246
  and intestacy, 53, 55
  insurance designations, 43–44, 46
  setting out trust provisions,
    175–77
  shareholders in private business,
    135, 136–37
  trusts for, 232
  unacknowledged, 129–33
mortgages, 232
multiple executors, 125–27
"my children" vs. legal children,
  94–95, 96

N
net worth, 28, 161, 162, 163, 201
non-binding memorandum, 152
Nova Scotia, will variation, 72
nursing homes, payments to, 33

O
Ontario, probate fees/taxes, 246
organizations, notifications to, 215
original will, 81–82, 94, 121, 123, 152
overcommunicating, 19
ownership, legal, 158–60

P
parents of deceased, and intestacy,
  49, 52
parents, first-time, 93

partnerships, 101
passwords, 121, 215
payments, stream of, 232
personal care decisions, categories,
  12–13 (*See also* power of attorney
  for personal care)
personal directives, xiv, 4–5, 242, 245
  communicating, 11, 13–15
  defined, 239, 245
  and end-of-life medical care, 17–20
  function of, 20
  legislation, 12
  defined, 225n, 245
  disappearances, 49, 207, 208, 225,
    226, 228
  executor role to secure, 207, 208
  and intestacy, 55, 57–58, 244
  storing, 227, 228
  tax on, 168
  value of, 57
  updating, 15
  vague, ambiguous, 18, 20
personal effects
  defined, 225n, 245
  disappearances, 49, 207, 208, 225,
    226, 228
  distribution tips, 227–28
  executor role to secure, 207, 208
  general transfer of, 150
  inadequately planning for
    distribution of, 149–52
  and intestacy, 55, 57–58, 244
  storing, 227, 228
  tax on, 168
  value of, 57, 227
philanthropy. *See* charitable giving
physicians, 22, 243